SENDING FORTH
LABORERS

A BIBLICAL HANDBOOK
FOR NEW TESTAMENT MISSIONS

DWIGHT TOMLINSON
& PAUL CHAPPELL

First published in 2007 by Striving Together Publications, a ministry of Lancaster Baptist Church, Lancaster, CA 93535. Striving Together Publications is committed to providing tried, trusted, and proven books that will further equip local churches to carry out the Great Commission. Your comments and suggestions are valued.

Striving Together Publications
4020 E. Lancaster Blvd.
Lancaster, CA 93535
800.201.7748

Cover design by Jeremy Lofgren
Layout by Craig Parker
Edited by Cary Schmidt
Special thanks to our proofreaders.

ISBN 978-1-59894-028-2

Printed in the United States of America

Table of Contents

FOREWORD

Sending Forth Laborers is a work that has been in the heart and mind of the two authors, Pastor Paul Chappell and Pastor Dwight Tomlinson for many years. About five years ago, Pastor Tomlinson began to communicate to me his burden to produce such a book. It is a joy to see this labor completed.

Both Pastor Chappell and Pastor Tomlinson are well qualified to write a book on missions. Both of them have had experience on foreign mission fields—Pastor Tomlinson served as a missionary in Hong Kong and established a good independent Baptist church, and Pastor Chappell lived in Korea as a missionary kid. Today, both men lead great missionary churches. They lead churches where missions is not just *a* program, but it is *the* program of the church. They are not only involved in sending laborers from their churches to the fields around the world, but they are heavily involved in supporting missionaries financially.

I am thrilled that good, independent Baptists are writing concerning this great endeavor. For too long, we have had to accept the works of men who give very little or no thought to the independent Baptist movement. There are at least ten thousand independent Baptist missionaries, and independent Baptist churches give approximately $400 million dollars every year to worldwide evangelization. Yet in most works, independent Baptists are not even mentioned; thus, it thrills my heart to see good material coming from the pens of godly men to the independent Baptist movement.

Looking at the four sections of this book thrills me. *The Missionary's Purpose*—his purpose is well stated in the four chapters on that subject. *Going to the Field*—how important it is that before young people go to the field, they consider the things these two good men have written. *Getting Settled on the Field*—if read and applied to the lives of new missionaries, these thoughts would prevent much attrition. The final and probably the most pertinent part of the book is *Doing the Work of a Missionary*. It is a shame that many missionaries—who have gone to the field, spent many years there, and returned to the States—had no idea what they were supposed to have done on the mission field. Just reading and applying the contents of this section would greatly enhance the effectiveness of independent Baptist missionaries.

I believe this book will be used in many ways. It will be a great asset to any local church. Every pastor should read this book. It will be a great asset for young pastors in guiding them to develop a biblically based missions church. This book will also be a great asset to missions teachers and Bible school students.

This book is biblical, practical, and good reading. I believe God has led these men in writing this book, and it will be a great blessing to all of us who utilize the contents.

DR. DON SISK
APRIL 2007

PREFACE

Worldwide missions is very much a team effort as given to us by Jesus and as seen in the model of first century Christianity. Pastors, local churches, Christians, and missionaries are called of God to strive together for the faith of the Gospel. We are called to accomplish the Great Commission together, and it takes every member of the team sharing the vision, understanding the philosophy, and obeying the Bible to make Christ's command to "teach all nations" a reality.

The book you hold in your hands is a very unique project for several reasons. This is a book written by men who clearly understand God's biblical instruction for world missions, and they also clearly understand the role of everybody "on the team." It is not often that you can read a book that gives such clear and practical instruction on such a vital subject. But it is even less likely that men who have served in so many facets of world missions would write such a book together.

Pastor Dwight Tomlinson, pastor of Liberty Baptist Church in Newport Beach, California, has served God effectively as a church planter both at home and on foreign soil. He intricately understands the faith, the sacrifice, the labor, and the biblical pattern of local church ministry as well as foreign missions.

Pastor Paul Chappell, pastor of Lancaster Baptist Church and President of West Coast Baptist College in Lancaster, California, grew up in local church ministries both in America and on foreign soil. He understands the unique lives of missionaries as well as pastors and local churches, and he has a great burden to touch the world with the Gospel.

Both men lead dynamic, growing Baptist churches with aggressive outreach ministries and large visions for worldwide missions. Both men are actively involved in speaking around the world, visiting foreign fields, and training missionaries for service. Both have served in advisory capacities to missions agencies and missionaries all over the world. They know the work of local churches, the needs of missionaries, and the challenges of pastoral work. They both have a personal heart for souls and a passion to send laborers into God's harvest fields.

More importantly, both of these men love missionaries. They both minister personally and regularly to missionaries and their families. They truly have a sincere heart to encourage Christian laborers around the world and to see the work of Christ increase.

These pages flow from minds that clearly understand the work of God from multiple perspectives and from hearts that truly love people. As you read, you will enjoy the practical ministry insight as well as the personal illustrations that take these principles from philosophy to reality. May God bless you and equip you to reach this world through the pages of this book!

INTRODUCTION

Have you ever noticed how gradual changes make big differences over long periods of time? This could be either good or bad, depending upon the nature of the shift and the circumstances in consideration. In recent years, we have seen a shift in the philosophy of New Testament missions in Christendom as well as in many fundamental churches.

While many may consider these shifts to be merely in methods or in response to cultural needs, we share a concern that these shifts run deeper than that. Our concern is that many are taking small steps away from the biblical principles that have sustained New Testament Missions for the past two thousand years. We believe over time, these shifts will result in far less being done for the work of Christ on foreign soil—unless we return to God's design.

The book you hold in your hands is our best effort to encourage fundamental, Christian missionaries to once again do the work of worldwide evangelization God's way. Regardless of pop culture, societal trends, and perceived needs, God's instructions to us are still very clear and His methods for preaching the Gospel and reaching the world still work. They work, if for no other reason than that they are God's. God's ways are not our ways, and His thoughts are not our thoughts. It never fails that when men try to do God's work their own way, the whole plan falls apart.

Yet, when Spirit-filled men of God choose to step out by faith and do God's work His way—even though it does not always make sense on paper—God empowers and blesses every time!

Perhaps you are a veteran missionary seeking to be reminded of why and how you are to carry out your life's calling. Perhaps you are a college student sensing a burden for missions and seeking to learn God's plan for the first time. Perhaps you are a pastor seeking to understand your role in reaching the world. Wherever this book finds you, we pray that these pages will equip you with a biblical philosophy and practical model of reaching the world.

In the coming chapters we would like to begin with the book of Acts and journey through God's plan for His local church to reach the world. We will see how first century Christianity raised up laborers, acknowledged God's call, trained servants for full-time ministry, sent them into the harvest, supported them in the work, heard their reports, and co-labored for the sake of the Gospel. We will rediscover the call, preparation, and plan of entering full-time missions work. We will also see the roles and responsibilities of supporting churches, sending churches, home pastors, and missions agencies. Every step of the journey will be biblically based and focused on the true purpose of missions—winning souls to Jesus Christ.

If you are seeking to discover or rediscover God's blueprint for worldwide evangelization, then keep reading. Let us begin making a shift back towards the Bible. Let us ask God to keep blessing first century Bible principles in the twenty-first century!

PART ONE

1

Preparing for Missions

CHAPTER ONE

The World's Need and God's Plan

Dwight Tomlinson

Picture a perfect world without any of the effects of sin to mar its beauty. No sin, disease, heartache, or death. There is no thorn to mar the beauty of the rose. The temperature is perfect, never too hot or cold. All of nature is in perfect harmony. The lion and the lamb play together in the fields. Not even a pesky mosquito mars the tranquility.

This is the world that God formed. A world of perfect beauty and harmony. Into this perfect world God placed His creation, beginning with plant life and ending with His crown jewel—man (Genesis 1:1–27). Adam and Eve lived in perfect harmony with nature, each other, and their Creator. They walked with God in beautiful fellowship. They had an important work to do as God's crowning act of creation. They were to care for the Garden of Eden and walk in fellowship with each other and God (Genesis 2:15). There was only one restriction placed upon them. They were granted permission to eat of the fruit of every tree in the garden except one—the tree of the knowledge of good and evil (Genesis 2:17). God wanted His people to know only good and not evil. God's plan for His creation has always been good. He knew that evil would mar the glory and peace of Eden; therefore, He prohibited Adam and Eve from eating the fruit of the one particular tree that would hurt them.

Time went by and Adam and Eve enjoyed a wonderful life just as God intended. The days were filled with taking care of the garden and playing with the animals that Adam had named; and each afternoon there was a special treat as God came to talk with them. We do not know how much time transpired, but that does not really matter. There were no board meetings and no deadlines screaming for their attention. The evenings were mild and joyful as Adam and Eve enjoyed the spectacular sunsets and then nestled together on a soft bed of grass more comfortable than any luxury hotel bed.

The day that paradise ended started as *any* other day. The birds serenaded Adam and Eve as they awoke to another perfect day, but before the sun set that evening everything had changed! That infamous day has gone down in history as the day that paradise was lost. In theological terms, we refer to it as "the fall of man." It is described in detail in the third chapter of Genesis. Satan came disguised as a beautiful serpent to tempt Eve.

He began by questioning the Word of God. "*…yea, hath God said, Ye shall not eat of every tree of the garden?*" (Genesis 3:1).

He continued with a flat-out lie, "*…Ye shall not surely die*" (vs. 4).

He then appealed to Eve's pride, convincing her that God was withholding something good from her. By the time it was over, Eve had disobeyed God, and Adam had done the same.

With this act of disobedience, the entire world was plunged into sin. Paradise was lost. From man's perspective Adam and Eve's sin might not seem especially significant. All they did was take a bite of some fruit. What made it serious was the fact that God had clearly commanded them not to taste of this particular fruit. This was the forbidden fruit of the tree of the knowledge of good and evil. Up to this point they were morally innocent. When they disobeyed God, they became by nature sinners. That moment they died spiritually and the physical process of dying began (Genesis 2:17). From Adam and Eve came every other human being who has ever lived upon the face of the earth. Thus Adam is the "federal head" from whom every other person has come. Adam and Eve became sinners before they conceived a child, and since we reproduce after our own kind, every human being is a sinner (Romans 5:12).

This sinful condition, which is the lot of all mankind, necessitates the central message of this book, and that is the subject of worldwide missions. Missions is simply the implementation of our Lord's Great Commission found in Matthew 28:18–20.

> *And Jesus came and spake unto them, saying, All power is given unto me in heaven and in earth. Go ye therefore, and teach all nations, baptizing them in the name of the Father, and of the Son, and of the Holy Ghost: Teaching them to observe all things whatsoever I have commanded you: and, lo, I am with you alway, even unto the end of the world. Amen.—MATTHEW 28:18–20*

The Great Commission was given to the New Testament church and is the privilege and responsibility of every church to fulfill. There is an aspect of missions that we sometimes overlook however, and that is the fact that the need of lost sinners alone is not our only motivation. It is true that men and women who die without Christ will spend eternity in Hell without hope. This truth should grip our hearts and send us out as compassionate evangelists; however, we must not lose sight of the fact that the battle in which we are engaged is a spiritual battle between God and the devil, between good and evil.

Why did the serpent come to Eve with his disgusting lies? We know that the serpent was actually Satan and the real reason he tempted Eve was because of his hatred for God (Genesis 3:1).

Satan of course was once an archangel who held a very high position in the angelic hierarchy. Satan was not content to serve in the exalted position that had been granted to him and for which he had been created. The creature was not content to love, worship, and serve the Creator. He desired worship himself. He wanted his throne to be exalted above the throne of God; therefore, he led a rebellion of the angelic creation against God. As a result of this rebellion, Satan and one third of the angels were cast out of Heaven. The once beautiful angel named Lucifer became the personification of evil whom we also know as the devil (see Isaiah 14).

When the devil showed up in the garden that day it was not really Adam and Eve that he wanted to destroy. It was the one who lovingly fashioned man from the dust of the earth and graciously formed a woman to be his soul mate that the devil wanted to hurt. Satan wounded Adam and Eve in an attempt to hurt God!

Satan could not touch the Lord God directly, but he knew that by attacking God's crowning act of creation, he could strike a blow that would be felt in the very heart of God. For as long as the devil has been the devil, it has been his diabolical scheme to hurt God by hurting those that He loves. He especially likes to accuse those who know the Lord Jesus Christ as their personal Saviour, for we are God's children by the new birth (Revelation 12:10).

What does all of this have to do with missions? Everything, for you see there is a battle going on that began thousands of years ago in the Garden of Eden. It is a battle for the souls of men and women who were created to glorify God. Will they lovingly submit to God, or will they follow the devil? The Lord Jesus Christ taught that we cannot serve two masters (Matthew 6:24). The context of that statement was serving God or money, but the principle applies to the discussion of serving Jesus or the devil.

The natural man is born into this world blinded by Satan and held captive by him through the desires of his own flesh (2 Corinthians 4:3–4). There is only one power that can set the captive free and bring him back to the God that loves him. That power is contained in the Gospel message of the death, burial and resurrection of Jesus Christ (Romans 1:16)!

The work of worldwide missions is all about getting that message to those who need to hear it. When Satan delivered his mortal blow to Adam and Eve in the garden, he wounded all of the nations of the world that would one day descend from them, thus creating the need for all nations to hear of the life-giving antidote.

Missions is God's method of the local church taking the antidote to the world. We have been commanded to do so, and we must not fail in this vital task (Matthew 28:18–20). What could be more important than taking the only message that can save a soul from Hell to a lost and dying world?

CHAPTER TWO

What Is It Going to Take to Reach the World?

Dwight Tomlinson

The Bible teaches that all men are lost and on their way to Hell without Jesus Christ. It says that there is only one way to be saved and that is by responding to the Gospel message in repentance and faith (Acts 20:21). The local church has been given the command to take the message to every creature, and God would not tell us to do something that we were not capable of doing. *"And he said unto them, Go ye into all the world, and preach the gospel to every creature"* (Mark 16:15). We *can do* what God has called us to do, but we cannot do it if we continue doing "what we have always done."

We need to return to the Word of God and to the God of the Word for answers in reaching this generation. This generation of Christians is going to answer to God for this generation of sinners. We will give an account for what we did with His plan—whether we obeyed it and implemented it according to His Word. We must return to the New Testament for both our *inspiration* and our *methodology*. Biblical methods such as fasting and praying need to be re-instituted as we obey God's plan in fulfilling the Great Commission.

God does not leave us to our own devices in obeying His will. Yes, it is true that He intends for us to use the brain He gave us. But our brain should be used to study His Word and to seek His wisdom, not to lean unto our own understanding without His guidance (Proverbs 3:5–6). In all matters related to reaching this world with the Gospel of Christ, God's Word must be our final authority—our roadmap for philosophy and methodology.

I firmly believe that modern day missions requires two biblical changes that we might be effective in carrying out God's Great Commission.

It Will Take a Change in Attitude

The Christian life is above all else a life of faith. We are saved by faith; we walk by faith; we serve by faith; and we must advance the Gospel by faith.

One of the first changes we need to make is to begin to *believe* by faith that we *can do* what God has commanded us to do. God desires for us to see people saved from every nation under Heaven, not just a few. Someday we will gather around His throne in Heaven, and when we do, He expects people to be there from every nation and every age in human history. In fact, He says that there will be people from every *"kindred, and tongue, and people, and nation"* (Revelation 5:9).

God desires to save people, and He will help us to propagate the Gospel if we will step out *by faith* and be serious about it— believing that it *can be* done! Quite simply, we will not get the message to every creature if we do not even believe it is possible.

Too often we are like the ten spies that brought back the negative report concerning the conquest of Canaan. Moses sent out twelve spies for the purpose of gathering information that would aid the Israelites in developing a battle plan for taking the land.

The spies returned, and only two had the faith to believe that the task could be completed. Ten of the twelve saw the giants and the obstacles as too great for them to overcome. Only Joshua and Caleb had the faith to believe that God would not command them to do something without giving them the ability to do it (Numbers 13–14)!

How about you? Do you *believe* that God will enable you to make a significant impact for world evangelization? Do you have enough faith to put your money, your resources, and even your whole life on the line? Do you really believe that He will enable you to make a difference in this world?

You may be thinking, "What could I possibly do to make a difference? There are billions of people on the earth today without Christ. How could I possibly even scratch the surface?" But you *can* make a difference. God is all-powerful, and if you are trusting in Him, He will unleash His power through you. He saved you for a purpose. You were created in Christ Jesus unto good works (Ephesians 2:10). You can do all things through Christ (Philippians 4:13)!

It is time that Christians have a change of attitude regarding world missions. Put your prayers, your finances, and your energy into world evangelism, *believing* that God will use you, and you will be amazed at what He will do through you.

It is said that Dwight Moody, while he was still a new Christian, heard a preacher say, "The world has yet to see what God can do through the life of one man completely yielded to Him." Young Mr. Moody was stirred in his soul that night, and he determined to be that man completely yielded to God. History has recorded for us the great revivals that accompanied Dwight Moody's ministry. By the grace of God he was used to shake America and England for Christ. The same God that used Moody wants to use you and me in our generation. By faith we must yield ourselves to Him and claim His blessings upon our efforts to reach the world!

The first thing that needs to change if we are to reach the world in our generation is our lack of faith in God. We must believe that God wants us to take seriously His commands and that He will help us if we step out in faith. Too often we say, "God, bless me and then I will believe," but that is not how God works. We say, "Let me see, and I will believe," but He replies, "No, believe, and you will see." That is exactly what Jesus told Martha at the gravesite of her brother Lazarus. If you will believe, you will see God's glory (John 11:40)!

Many years ago a young man of humble background and means had a God-given desire to take the Gospel to the unreached peoples of Burma. Adoniram Judson was convinced that there was only one way for people to be saved and that was through the Lord Jesus Christ. Judson and his fellow Baptists decided that they would step out by faith to get the Gospel to Burma. They concentrated on winning men to Christ and planting churches in Burma. As a result of their faith and God's blessings, today there are over 200,000 Christians that meet to worship God in those churches! God is just as willing to bless our faithful labor as He was for Adoniram Judson.

God has allowed me to start three different churches; two in America, and one in Hong Kong, China. All three churches were started by faith. I believed that God would bless my efforts, and He did. I do not say that in an arrogant way. I understand that I am nothing outside of Christ. But I also understand something else— the ministry is not about me, it is about Him! He is the one with the power, and He works through imperfect human vessels like you and me. We must get our eyes off what we *do not* have and instead focus on what He *does* have. We will never reach the world if we sit around complaining about ourselves and our limitations. The King of the universe is looking for some people to believe that He wants to bless and use them. I believe that I am one of the people that He is looking for, and I believe that you are as well. Let us get rid of our evil hearts of unbelief and start believing that God says what He means and means what He says.

It Will Take a Change in Methodology

Not only does our attitude of unbelief need to change, but we also must return to biblical methods.

I realize that we are living in the twenty-first century, but I do not believe we should look to the twenty-first century to develop a strategy for missions. Following a twenty-first century map will lead us to a twenty-first century destination. The church of the twenty-first century is described by Jesus Christ as lukewarm and nauseating (Revelation 3:14–16)—not exactly what we are looking for in a church that changes the world.

We need to look not to the twenty-first century church, but to the first century church. Roman governor Plinius Secundus wrote in his *Epistles x96* that Christians were people who loved the truth *at any cost*. Although he was ordered to torture and execute them for refusing to curse Jesus, he was continually amazed and impressed with their firm commitments "not to do any wicked deeds, never to commit any fraud, theft, adultery, never to falsify their word, not to deny a trust when they should be called upon to deliver it up." For centuries, true Christians around the world have stood as shining examples of the standards of truth and love established by Jesus Christ.

Historian Philip Schaff described the overwhelming influence which Jesus had on subsequent history and culture of the world: "This Jesus of Nazareth, without money and arms, conquered more millions than Alexander, Caesar, Mohammed, and Napoleon; without science…he shed more light on things human and divine than all philosophers and scholars combined; without the eloquence of schools, he spoke such words of life as were never spoken before or since, and produced effects which lie beyond the reach of orator or poet; without writing a single line, he set more pens in motion, and furnished themes for more sermons, orations, discussions, learned volumes, works of art, and songs of praise than the whole army of great men of ancient and modern times."

What were the methods of the first century church? What strategy did the first followers of Jesus Christ adopt that made them so effective in their attempt to win souls? How is it that the enemies of the Gospel were compelled to say about our forefathers in the faith, "...*These that have turned the world upside down are come hither also*" (Acts 17:6)?

It was not their positive, non-offensive, seeker-friendly, come-as-you-are message that caused the world to be turned upside down. We know this because the same people who accused the early Christians of making such a change also felt that the Christians were holding them responsible for killing God's Son! "They intend to bring His blood upon our heads," they cried out.

The first century church witnessed with such power that all the legions of Hell were not able to stop the forward motion of the Gospel! What began as a small sect with about 120 adherents in an upper room in Jerusalem, spread like wildfire until within one generation, it filled the great Roman Empire! How is it that one small church with humble fishermen as its leaders were able to make such a dramatic impact upon their world? Never before had so few accomplished so much with so little. Perhaps the real question should be, how is it that so many, with so much, are doing so little today? I believe that we must get back to first century, biblical methods if we ever expect to see first century results. Let us consider some first century methods and recommit ourselves to putting God's original plan to work in a twenty-first century world.

The early church sought the filling of the Holy Spirit through prayer.

Acts 1 records that Jesus told His disciples to wait in Jerusalem until they were endued with power by the Holy Spirit, after which they were to commence telling the world about Him (Acts 1:8).

It is a fairly simple, unsophisticated strategy, but they obeyed. They went to Jerusalem, entered into a ten-day prayer meeting, and on the day of Pentecost the Holy Spirit came just as Jesus had promised. They were filled with the Holy Spirit and given a miraculous ability to preach in languages they had not learned. The purpose of the miracle was to enable the multitudes of visitors in Jerusalem that day to understand the Gospel message. As a result of their Spirit-filled preaching, three thousand souls were saved, baptized, and added to the church in one day! I am not against strategizing or considering new methods as long as they do not violate the principles of Scripture. But, I cannot help but believe that we would be better off if we returned to some old-fashioned prayer meetings instead.

The church was empowered in a prayer meeting, not a rock concert. There was no "praise and worship" band to entertain the congregation. There were no "feel-good" or "how-to" seminars to which the members were encouraged to invite their friends to come and learn how to be healthy, wealthy, and happy. They were simply a church on their face before God, confessing sin and praying for God to use them to reach their city!

I understand that the day of Pentecost in Acts chapter two will never be repeated. Days similar to Pentecost returned another thirty times in the book of Acts, yet the miraculous events of chapter two were never repeated. My point is not that we need the details to be repeated, but that we need to get back to fasting and praying for the power of God to fall upon us once again! We must have His mighty power that we might impact our world just as the first generation

Christians did. Prayer was as natural to the first century churches as potlucks and barbecues are to today's churches.

As we look through the history of the church, prayer has always been a key factor in missions. The missionary movement as we know it today was born in Acts chapter thirteen in Antioch of Syria. The leaders of the church had called for a period of fasting and praying, and it was during that time of waiting upon God that the Holy Spirit called the first missionaries (Acts 13:1–4).

The church was empowered in a prayer meeting. The missions movement began in a prayer meeting. The testimony of history is that when the church gets serious about prayer, God hears and honors her prayers. Many examples could be cited, but consider the following example taken from *Key to the Missionary Problem* written by Andrew Murray.

Moravia was a province in the northwest of the Austrian Empire. In the fifteenth century it was the scene of horrible persecution perpetrated by the Roman Catholic church. John Huss was burned at the stake there for preaching the Gospel in 1415. Many Bible-believing Christians were martyred as a result of their refusal to bow the knee to the Roman persecutors. Some of those who remained faithful to Christ gathered in a valley in the neighboring province of Bohemia. There in 1457, they became known as "The Brethren of the Law of Christ." At the turn of the century, the Pope and the King combined against them with the intent of complete annihilation. Their persecution continued until in 1548, a Royal Edict drove thousands of them to Poland where a large and prosperous church was formed. With a new King, in 1556, peace returned, and the Brethren's church was again firmly established and divided into the three provinces of Bohemia, Moravia, and Poland.

With the accession of Fredrick II, everything suddenly changed. The Day of Blood at Prague in 1620, witnessed the execution of twenty-seven of their leaders. During the six years that followed,

Bohemia was a field of blood and the Brethren Church was almost destroyed. During the whole century those who stayed in the country worshipped God in secret. John Amos Comenius, the last bishop of the church in Moravia, wrote in 1660: "Experience clearly teaches that particular churches are sometimes destroyed by the hand of God stretched out in wrath. Yet other churches are either planted in their stead, or the same churches rise in other places. Whether God will deem her worthy to be revived in her native land, or let her die there and resuscitate her elsewhere, we know not…according to His own promise, the Gospel will be brought by those Christians who have been justly chastened, to the remaining peoples of the earth; and thus, as of old, our fall will be the riches of the world."

In 1707, another of their leaders, George Jaeschke, spoke similar words. On his deathbed at the age of eighty-three, he spoke, "It may seem as if the final end of the Brethren's Church has come. But my beloved children, you will see a great deliverance. The remnant will be saved. I do not know whether this deliverance will come to pass here in Moravia, or whether you will have to go out of 'Babylon'; but I do know that it will transpire not very long hence. I am inclined to believe that an exodus will take place, and that a refuge will be offered on a spot where you will be able, without fear, to serve the Lord according to His Holy Word."

The Lord indeed provided a place of refuge. In 1722, Count Nicholas Louis Von Zinzendorf granted permission to bring refugees from Moravia to his estate in Saxony. Ten reached Berthelsdorf in June of 1722. Before long, two hundred had gathered on the spot allocated to them. They called their settlement Herrnhut—The Lord's Watch. They took the word in its double meaning: the watch of the Lord *over them*; the watch of the Lord to be kept *by them* in prayer.

Herrnhut became a refuge for the persecuted. All sorts of displaced Christians came to seek a home there. On May 12, 1727, just five years after the first arrival of ten persons, Count Zinzendorf called together the group, which now numbered three hundred. He read to them a list of statutes that had been drawn up to govern how they lived. There was to be no more discord. Brotherly love and unity in Christ were to be the golden chains that bound them together. All of the people pledged themselves to obey the statutes. That day was the beginning of new life in Herrnhut.

Twenty-one years later on May 12, 1748, the Count wrote these words: "Today, twenty-one years ago, the fate of Herrnhut hung in the balance, whether it was to become a sect, or to take its place in the church of our Saviour. After an address of three or four hours, the power of the Holy Spirit decided for the latter. What the Saviour did after that, up to the winter, cannot be expressed. The whole place was indeed a veritable dwelling of God with men; and on the 13 of August it passed into continual praise. It then quieted down, and entered the Sabbath rest."

After the statutes had been adopted, the spirit of fellowship and prayer was greatly increased. It is said that prayer was often in such power that those present were either convicted and changed, or felt compelled to leave. All night prayer meetings became commonplace. The whole congregation was conscious of an overwhelming power in their midst. Soulwinning in the surrounding neighborhoods became very important to the church.

On August 22, it was recorded: "Today, we considered how needful it is that our church, which is yet in her infancy and has in Satan such a mighty enemy, should guard herself against one who never slumbers day nor night, and have an unceasing holy watch kept against him. We resolved, therefore, to light a freewill offering of intercession which should burn night and day...."

In the course of the following months some of the Brethren were continually traveling to places near and far, preaching the Gospel of Christ. At a meeting on February 10, 1728, the Count spoke to the church of the need in distant lands. He spoke especially of Turkey, Morocco, and Greenland.

The following four years were times of continual revival. The prayer meetings continued, as well as the jealous maintenance of the spirit of brotherly love and the efforts to take the Gospel to more and more distant regions. It is said that in the first twenty years of its existence, this congregation actually sent out more missionaries than all the rest of the churches sent out in two hundred years!

I cannot help but wonder what would happen today if our churches got back to the New Testament injunctions of prayer and the filling of the Spirit. Perhaps it would not take missionaries two or three years to raise their support and get to the field. I suspect that our missions giving would see a dramatic increase, as would every other area of spirituality in our churches.

The early church made a commitment of personnel and finances.

One of the hindrances to world evangelization in this generation is the widespread materialism of the day. As Americans we enjoy the most lavish and rich lifestyle the world has ever seen. We are so prosperous that we have come to see financial gain as a God-given right. It is easy for even good Christian people to become more concerned with the accumulation of wealth than with evangelizing the world. After all, we are a part of a society that places great importance on having the things that only money can buy—driving the right car, living in the right neighborhood, buying the right clothes, etc. None of these things are intrinsically wrong, but they can become more important to us than God ever intended them to be. Our satisfaction should come from our relationship to God, not the amount of money in our bank accounts.

If we are going to get the Gospel to the world in our generation, we must be willing to give of both our lives and our substance. Materialism does not only show itself in selfishness when it comes to giving money, but also in our attitudes in giving our children to the work of God. For example, many Christian parents discourage their children from attending Bible college, opting instead to send them to accredited state colleges and universities. I am not saying that it is always wrong to attend a state university, or that every Christian young person should attend Bible college. But I am afraid that far too often the motivation behind where our young people attend school has nothing to do with the will of God and everything to do with perceived future financial gain!

Every Christian young person should be taught that it is his or her duty and privilege to seek God's will concerning full-time service. Obviously not all will be called to missions, but all should make it a matter of serious prayer. Those who are not called to go must understand that they are called to send. The Great Commission is for *every* child of God, and it requires that we either go ourselves or help send those who do go (Matthew 28:18–20).

The Bible teaches that the first century Christians understood their privilege of both going *themselves* and sending *others*. Even a casual reading of the book of Acts would lead us to the conclusion that not only the apostles, but the ordinary church members were taking every opportunity to give out the Gospel. The first local church met in Jerusalem, and they filled that city with the message of the death, burial and resurrection of their Lord (Acts 5:28).

When persecution came and the church members were scattered, the Bible tells us that they continued soulwinning and witnessing everywhere they went (Acts 8:4). Remember it was not the pastors who left Jerusalem, but the ordinary members. Soulwinning has never been something just for the pastor or staff member. The early Christians understood that they had the responsibility and privilege of telling others about Christ. The church at Thessalonica was so effective at spreading the Gospel that they witnessed to people all over their area. *"For from you sounded out the word of the Lord not only in Macedonia and Achaia, but also in every place your faith to*

God-ward is spread abroad; so that we need not to speak any thing" (1 Thessalonians 1:8). You could not find anyone who lived in their area that had not heard the Gospel at least once. In fact, Paul said that they were so zealous in witnessing that it was not necessary for him to send anymore workers there!

Not only did the early church members win souls themselves and gladly give their members as missionaries, but they also put their money into spreading the Gospel. I am not talking about just the rich. Some of the early believers were very poor, yet they gave joyfully and generously to the work of God. They did not have a "poor me, I can not afford to give" attitude. In fact, they understood that giving was a great privilege and that it was through giving that God would be able to bless them financially (see 2 Corinthians 8:1–4 and 9:6).

As Christians, we must put our money to work in winning the world to Christ. Tithing is the beginning point of Christian giving, but it should not be the stopping point. God has promised to bless those who give generously to His work. Every Christian should tithe ten percent of his income to their local church and then give offerings above that. It is my belief that "faith promise missions" is the best method of supporting missions today.

Reaching the world with the Gospel of Christ requires that we return to the first century model of the local church. This model began with believers trusting God—believing that it can be done and that God will enable us by His power. Then we must once again fall to our knees and seek God's filling and power. His Holy Spirit is our only source of power—far above strategies and methods. Finally, a first century model requires that we each actively participate in the Great Commission—both by going personally and sharing the Gospel everywhere we go, and by giving a portion of our substance toward reaching the world.

Though the twenty-first century church seems to be forever experimenting with failing methods and contemporary ideas,

God's original plan still works! If we will return to biblical methods and the Holy Spirit's power, we can make a difference in reaching our world for Christ—God promises so!

CHAPTER THREE

Missionary Qualifications

Dwight Tomlinson

B*ut in a great house there are not only vessels of gold and of silver, but also of wood and of earth; and some to honour, and some to dishonour. If a man therefore purge himself from these, he shall be a vessel unto honour, sanctified, and meet for the master's use, and prepared unto every good work.*—2 Timothy 2:20–21

The work of a foreign missionary has never been easy, but it is a work well worth the sacrifices required. Stephen Neil wrote in *Builders of the Indian Church*:

"I may place on record my conviction that the needs of the mission field are always greater than the needs of the church at home, that no human qualifications, however high, render a man or woman more than adequate for missionary work, that there is no career that affords such scope for enterprise and creative work, and that in comparison with the slight sacrifice demanded, the reward is great beyond all measuring."

The modern missions movement among independent Baptist churches can be traced all the way back to Acts 13. We will analyze this chapter in detail in future chapters, but right now I want to simply draw the reader's attention to the fact that there were definite qualifications for the first missionaries sent out by local churches.

First and foremost, there must be a love for Jesus Christ that compels the Christian to give his life in sacrificial service to his Lord. Judas (not the infamous Iscariot) and Silas were two such missionaries in the first century. They were men whose hearts had been taken captive by the love of Christ. They were willing to follow Jesus anywhere and pay any price for which His service called. They were described by their peers as men that hazarded their lives for the name of Jesus Christ (Acts 15:25–27).

Second, a missionary must have a divine calling. Missions is not a profession that one chooses as he would a secular job. It is a divine calling. It was while the church at Antioch was engaged in serving the Lord and fasting that the Holy Ghost laid upon their hearts the names of two missionaries. In Acts 13:2, the Bible says, *"As they ministered to the Lord, and fasted, the Holy Ghost said, Separate me Barnabas and Saul for the work whereunto I have called them."* The Holy Spirit did not say, "Choose two men that you think would be well suited for this type of work." The man or woman who sets out to serve Jesus Christ as a foreign missionary must have a deep sense of calling. It is this calling that will enable them to endure the many hardships and discouragements of missionary life.

If the missionary candidate is married, there must be complete agreement between husband and wife that this is indeed the will of God for their lives. A wife should accept and be supportive of God's call in her husband's life. It would be very unwise for a husband to pressure his wife into moving to a foreign country and culture if she is not convinced of God's leading. A husband and wife should have a close enough relationship to each other and the Lord that they can follow His leading together.

Third, the missionary candidate should be doctrinally grounded before going to the field. The new missionary is going to have to preach in churches while raising his support. He must be able to biblically present the case for worldwide missions. He is asking the local church to make him an extension of their ministry. It is imperative that he be able to articulate his doctrinal beliefs and support them with the Word of God. It is not enough to simply say that you love Jesus and that people need to be saved. There is more in the Bible than salvation. The Great Commission contains much more than salvation. The Lord Jesus Christ commanded His church to not only bring people to salvation, but also to baptize and teach them (Matthew 28:18–20).

A missionary must be able to teach his new converts the great doctrines of the Word of God. It is only by the Word of God that newborn babes in Christ can be expected to grow into mature followers of Christ. First Peter 2:2 says, *"As newborn babes, desire the sincere milk of the word, that ye may grow thereby."* In my opinion, if a missionary candidate does not have a clear understanding of basic Bible doctrines, he should not attempt to go to the field. Every missionary must know what he believes and why. Let me suggest a list that I would consider a minimum knowledge base for an independent Baptist missionary.

> The Doctrine of God
> The Doctrine of the Holy Spirit
> The Doctrine of the Virgin Birth
> The Doctrine of the Deity of Christ
> The Doctrine of Salvation
> The Doctrine of the Church
> The Doctrines of Heaven and Hell
> The Doctrine of the Second Coming of Christ
> The Doctrine of the Inspiration of Scripture
> The Doctrine of Separation
>   (Both Ecclesiastical and Personal)

I believe that these would be the absolute minimum that a missionary should be able to clearly explain with an open Bible. In addition to these basic Bible doctrines, the missionary should be able to preach and teach the church's responsibility and privilege of being involved in worldwide missions.

We must send men to the mission field that can win souls and plant churches. It might be possible for a person going on a short-term trip to be a little unsettled on doctrine, but that luxury cannot be afforded a church planter. A person may go to the field and assist the missionary without understanding why he or she is a Baptist, but the man who is charged by God to preach the Word, had better study to show himself approved in this great work!

Fourth, there should be a measure of success in the ministry at home before going to the foreign field. I do not believe it is wise for a missionary to go to the foreign field without first having at least a measure of success and experience in serving the Lord through his local church.

> *But let every man prove his own work, and then*
> *shall he have rejoicing in himself alone, and not in*
> *another.*— Galatians 6:4

The day has long since gone that you will be respected and followed just because you are an American. I well remember the day I sat with a group of Filipino and Korean pastors who said to me with heavy hearts, "Please do not send us one more novice that is going to demand that we follow him just because of the color of his skin!" These men were not being critical of America, neither were they rejecting missionaries. They were simply being asked to be treated as equals and coworkers for Christ. These were men who loved missionaries and appreciated all that America had done for the physical and spiritual welfare of their countries, but they felt that it was unfair to be expected to follow someone's leadership just because he happened to be born into a country that is richer than the rest of the world.

I must admit that I agree. Being a citizen of a particular nation does not automatically endue one with spiritual authority. The Bible is clear that spiritual leadership must be earned, not demanded.

I had the privilege of serving my country in the United States Army during the Vietnam Conflict. I served two tours in Vietnam and found that the most respected officers in combat are those who have proven themselves worthy by being engaged in the battle. The most respected leaders are those who know what it is like to be on the front lines. It is not "shake and bake" tin soldiers who have never known the fear or the agony of battle that receive the respect and loyalty of their fellow soldiers. We need men in leadership whose hands are calloused by labor and whose hearts have been touched by the fire of the Holy Ghost! Theodore Roosevelt said it much more eloquently than I can.

> It is not the critic who counts, not the man who points out how the strong man stumbles, or where the doer of deeds could have done them better. The credit belongs to the man who is actually in the arena, whose face is marred by dust and sweat and blood; who errs, and comes short again and again; who knows the great enthusiasms, the great devotions, who spends himself in a worthy cause; who at best, knows in the end the triumph of high achievement, and who at the worst if he fails, at least fails while doing greatly, so that his place shall never be with those cold and timid souls who know neither victory nor defeat.

May God raise up some men whose faces are marred by dust, sweat, and blood even before they arrive on the mission field. Mission agencies and local churches differ on the amount of experience a man should have before being accepted as a part of their missionary family. Some agencies require a certain number of years of full-time ministry or internship before granting the missionary approved status. Others require simply a clear salvation testimony, basic doctrinal agreement, local church sponsorship, and a verbal testimony of the call to the field. My point is not to argue with anyone who is sincerely trying to help God-called men get to the field. Let each missionary and each church or agency be fully persuaded in their own mind that they are following the plan of God for them.

My argument is not from a policy position but a practical one. It just does not make sense that the first time a missionary engages in spiritual warfare would be when he arrives on the foreign field. The great missionary statesman, Hudson Taylor, understood this. He recorded his struggles of faith before he ever went to China. God had called him to China, but he knew that he must learn to trust God back home in England if he was ever to trust God in the faraway land of China. How could he serve God in China, trusting completely in Christ if he had not first learned to serve and trust Him at home?

What qualifies a man to plant churches on the mission field? He must have a passionate love for Jesus Christ, an undeniable life-calling from God, a solid understanding of biblical doctrine, and a measure of success in ministry here at home. A committed life, a called heart, an educated mind, and a proven track record—these are the four primary qualifications that I believe God will bless as we seek to send those upon whom God has placed His hand.

CHAPTER FOUR

The Preparation of the Missionary

Dwight Tomlinson

Church history is filled with examples of great missionaries. Each of them has a story of the grace of God working in their lives preparing them for sacrificial service on the foreign field. An important part of any missionary's preparation should be reading biographies of those great missionaries who have gone before. Biographies of great Baptists such as William Carey, Adoniram Judson, and others will inspire and instruct us as we seek to also be used of God.

One of the greatest missionaries of all time was the Apostle Paul. He was a man that was prepared by God for his missionary work, and we can profit greatly by considering how God prepared him for missionary service. In fact, we are told in Scripture that God saved Paul and raised him up as a pattern for us to follow (see 1 Timothy 1:16).

How did God prepare Paul to become the great missionary that he was? Are there any principles that will help us as we seek to prepare ourselves or others to serve in this noble calling?

The Bible always has the answers. It is our guidebook, and we can always turn to its inspired pages to find the light that we need to guide us through the darkness.

Paul did not automatically become a great missionary. He went through the same process of preparation that is needed today, beginning with his own conversion and baptism and continuing through mentoring and grounding in local church ministry. Let us briefly consider how God helped Paul to grow to the point that he could be chosen as the first local church missionary.

Paul Prepared by Serving in the Local Church

The conversion of Paul is recorded in Acts 9. His Jewish name was Saul and is used in the Scripture up to Acts 13:9, after which he is referred to by his Roman name Paul. It is significant that within three days of his conversion Saul had followed Christ in water baptism and identified with the church at Damascus. The local church is God's ordained institution for the propagation of the Gospel. It is also the institution through which new converts are to be nurtured in the faith. Every new convert should become involved in a local church and that involvement should continue for his or her entire life.

Some years later, God led Saul to the city of Jerusalem. The first thing he did was attempt to affiliate with the church there. He ran into a problem however, that the church did not believe he was really saved! They were concerned that the former persecutor was simply trying to join the church in order to be in a better position to persecute believers.

From Jerusalem Saul went to Tarsus, and from Tarsus he was taken by Barnabas to the church at Antioch, where once again he became involved in faithful service through the church. This became the pattern of his life. He was always either planting churches where they did not exist, or finding the disciples that already existed and meeting with them. The local church was the training ground for the greatest missionary that ever lived, and it is still the best place to be trained!

Paul Prepared by Spending Time Alone with Jesus

There were two periods in Saul's life that were what might be called silent years. When he first left Damascus as a new convert, he did not immediately go to Jerusalem. There was a three-year period spent in the Arabian desert getting to know his new Lord. Many years later he wrote in the book of Galatians about that time. He said that it was during that desert time alone with God that the Lord revealed to him the Gospel of the grace of God (Galatians 1:10–18).

Another silent time in Saul's life was when he first left Jerusalem and returned to his hometown of Tarsus. There were several years that transpired before Barnabas came seeking Saul to take him to view the new Gentile church in Antioch (Acts 11:25–26).

God has not chosen to reveal all that was happening in Saul's life during those silent years, but I think it is safe to surmise that Saul was getting to know God in a more intimate way. He was no doubt studying the Old Testament Scriptures and becoming convinced that the Lord Jesus Christ was indeed the promised Jewish Messiah. He was learning the importance of prayer and fasting and waiting on God. Time spent alone with God is never wasted; in fact, it is absolutely vital for success in the ministry. The missionary must be above all else a man that knows God intimately.

Do not be discouraged if God has a "desert training time" for you. The greatest man of the Old Testament was Moses and the greatest missionary of the New Testament was Paul. Both of them had a period of desert training, getting to know God before they did great things for Him!

Paul Prepared by Serving As An Apprentice to Barnabas

As a young convert Saul was influenced and trained by Barnabas. Every new convert needs someone like Barnabas who will take him under his wing and show him how to live the Christian life. God's plan is that Christianity be a religion of "show and tell." It is not enough to tell people that they should serve God; we need to be continually bringing people alongside us and demonstrating how to serve. This was the method that Barnabas used with the new convert Saul, and it became the method that Saul later adopted as the great Apostle Paul. It was also the method he instructed his converts to use.

> *And the things that thou hast heard of me among*
> *many witnesses, the same commit thou to faithful*
> *men, who shall be able to teach others also.*
> —2 Timothy 2:2

In this verse we see God's plan of show and tell. Barnabas had taught Paul how to serve God, and Paul had taught Timothy to serve God. Timothy was now to commit the precious truths of the Word of God to faithful men, and they in turn were to teach others. This transfer of knowledge and training was not to be done in isolation but "among many witnesses."

The best training ground is the local church. That is not to say that there is something wrong with an institution dedicated to training young men and women to serve God full time, but that institution should never be divorced from the local church. In my opinion, the best Bible colleges are those that are either operated by, or closely affiliated with a local church. An institution that hopes to train leaders of churches should at the very least require its students to be active, serving members of a local church.

Barnabas took Saul as an apprentice and worked with him in three local churches—Damascus, Jerusalem, and Antioch. They went together on the first missionary journey where they planted churches. It was on this missions trip that the Lord moved the leadership from Barnabas to Saul, and the name Paul began to be used instead of Saul.

We may glean from the actions of Barnabas, the New Testament Scriptures, and Paul's own ministry that we should be continually training young men and women through the local church to serve God. Every pastor should make it a priority to dedicate much of his time, prayer and energy to producing holiness in the lives of the young people in his church.

A young man that feels called into the Gospel ministry would be wise to latch onto a godly, older pastor and glean all that he could from him. The wisest man who ever lived said, *"He that walketh with wise men shall be wise: but a companion of fools shall be destroyed"* (Proverbs 13:20).

This can be an invaluable part of preparing for a great ministry.

We have seen three biblical principles for preparation from Paul's life. First, a missionary must prepare by serving in a local church. Second, a missionary must prepare by spending time alone with Christ. Third, a missionary must prepare through mentoring relationships with other godly ministry leaders. This is God's pattern in the New Testament, which simply means there is no better pattern for preparing for the work of Christ.

PART TWO

2

Going to the Field

CHAPTER FIVE

The Sending Church

PAUL CHAPPELL

G od has given us a plan for reaching the world through the ministry of the local New Testament church. Contrary to the ideas of many, this is God's "Plan A," and He has no "Plan B." I thank God that He has used many parachurch ministries to reach lost souls; however, even parachurch workers would be the first to admit that without the local church, there is no remaining fruit to their evangelism strategies.

Any honest student of the Bible will quickly acknowledge that the only biblical "sending agency" for missionaries is the local church. While we thank God for missions boards or missions agencies that assist local churches in the work, there can be no substitute for the local church as the sending agency of a missionary.

As a pastor of a local Baptist church, I have often recommended missionaries for support who were sent by their churches in affiliation with one group or another. I am not an anti-missions board pastor. My only concern is that the missions boards always realize their place is to serve the local churches and their missionaries by helping them in the areas of insurance, legal visa work, banking, mailings, etc. I do not believe missions boards should replace the local church as the sending agent.

Biblical Description of the Local Church

In Acts 13 we find a blueprint for world missions in the church at Antioch—one of the most dynamic churches of the first century. I believe the church at Antioch could be called the "cradle of New Testament missions."

In Acts 13:1 the Bible says, "*Now there were in the church that was at Antioch certain prophets and teachers….*" The word *church* as it is used here means "a called out assembly" or those "summoned for a definite purpose." These were the saved, baptized believers of the church at Antioch. The prophets and teachers taught and preached the Word of God to new believers who were growing in the grace and knowledge of the Lord Jesus Christ. Undoubtedly, these believers received their missionary zeal from the teaching and preaching they heard in that place.

One of the key leaders in this church was Barnabas. He was an encouraging and equipping pastor. We need more Barnabas-like pastors today who will equip people for the work of the ministry, including worldwide missions. Barnabas was obviously a spiritual leader with a passion for souls and a passion to develop others.

The church at Antioch was not only a church with a great spiritual testimony and godly leaders, but it was also a church with a hungering to know the will of God. This is evidenced in Acts 13:2, where the Bible says they were ministering to the Lord and fasting. Fasting is the denial of self in order to bring prayer to its fullest development. From this principle we see that a sending church must be willing to sacrifice in order to know God and to fulfill His Great Commission.

It was to this church that the Holy Ghost said, "*Separate me Barnabas and Saul for the work whereunto I have called them.*" Sometimes I wonder if the average church today would hear the Holy Spirit when He is calling forth laborers into the harvest field. I believe many churches have lost their sensitivity to the leading of the Lord in this area.

It has been a great joy to see godly men sent forth from Lancaster Baptist Church who are pastoring as near as Los Angeles and as far away as St. Petersburg, Russia. These were vital, soulwinning, tithing men of God who were members of our local body, yet God called them to preach the Gospel of Jesus Christ. I thank the Lord that they were willing to hear the Holy Spirit's call and that our church was privileged to send them forth.

Perhaps one of the most critical verses to comprehend regarding the concept of sending forth laborers is found in Acts 13:3 where the Bible says, "*And when they had fasted and prayed, and laid their hands on them, **they sent them away.***" Who are "they" in verse three? Obviously, this is referring to the believers in Antioch. It was this local body who sent away Paul and Barnabas on the first missionary journey.

Sadly, we have many bureaucratic institutions in Christendom that have overcomplicated the simplicity of New Testament evangelism and missions. In this passage we simply see a church sending two men to go forward with the Gospel. This was a sacred and spiritual action, and it should be the pattern for all world evangelism today.

Having been sent forth by the local church, the Bible says they "*departed unto Seleucia; and from thence they sailed to Cyprus*" (verse 4). From this, we understand that the first missionary journey to Seleucia was about a sixteen-mile trip. As Paul traveled on to Salamis, he was joined there by a young man named John Mark. Traveling to the isle of Paphos, the first missionaries encountered a sorcerer—a false prophet—whose name was Bar-jesus.

Immediately, in reading the biblical text, we see and sense the need for prayerful and financial support. These men would need help and encouragement from the local church as they fought the spiritual warfare that world missions requires.

I recall coming to Lancaster in 1986. Our family had no salary, and the church had only a few families. Within the first two weeks of moving to this Southern California town, the church was broken into and the few possessions we had, stolen. In addition, during our second day in this city, I was out soulwinning, and a lady came into our home and had an epileptic seizure while screaming at my wife.

Day after day, we met spiritual resistance in establishing this new work; However, thanks to the prayers and financial support of a few dozen churches, we were sustained, and a church was planted to the glory of God.

What a great blessing it is to read in verse twelve, "*Then the deputy, when he saw what was done, believed, being astonished at the doctrine of the Lord.*" Here we see a deputy of Caesar now accepting Jesus Christ as Saviour. All of this is because a church was willing to send forth the first two missionaries in obedience to the Word of God.

Later in Acts 14:26–28 the Bible teaches that Paul and Barnabas returned to Antioch. We read, "*And thence sailed to Antioch, from whence they had been recommended to the grace of God for the work which they fulfilled. And when they were come, and had gathered the church together, they rehearsed all that God had done with them, and how he had opened the door of faith unto the Gentiles. And there they abode long time with the disciples.*"

Here we see the cycle of local church missions. We have seen a church obey the Holy Spirit and missionaries yield to the Holy Spirit and go to the regions beyond. After a period of four or five years, the missionaries returned to the sending church and rehearsed with them all that God had done through their efforts.

One cannot read Acts 13 and 14 without sensing the dynamic relationship between the missionaries and the local church. It was one that was spiritual, sacrificial, and highly accountable.

In recent days, I have seen some men claim to be "local church" missionaries who were not accountable to local congregations or their local pastors. It was as if this less cumbersome way of going to the mission field had granted them, in their own minds, a liberty not to give a report or not be as accountable as others. This lack of accountability is neither scriptural nor healthy. God's model requires a local church and a missionary working in close cooperation for world missions.

Perhaps some missions agencies have been overly involved in demanding accountability. Yet there are others that assist the local church pastors in their support of dozens of missionaries. These organizations provide standardized financial policies and moral guidelines, as well as systems of reporting and accountability to local churches that support the biblical model.

It is my opinion that the local pastor should have policies and standards for missionaries, but it may be that a local pastor will find confidence in cooperating with a missions board with similar policies and standards. This relationship can be profitable for the encouragement of missionaries and for the integrity of the missions process.

However this relationship develops, let no one mistake the fact that it is the local church that is spiritually, morally, and financially accountable for the sending of the missionary. As we do not believe Christian parents should delegate their responsibilities for child-rearing to the Christian school or youth group, even so, the local church pastor should not feel that the missions agency is solely responsible for the spiritual oversight of the missionary. This is simply not biblical. God always blesses His plan, and we must make sure we carry out His commands in accordance with His instructions.

Practical Helps for the Missionary

Besides being a spiritual sending agency for the missionary, the local church should do everything within its power to help the missionary and his family accomplish the work God has led them to do. There are several ways a pastor and local church can be a blessing to the missionary.

First, we must provide financial support. A sending church should be the largest supporting church, financially, of the missionary. If it is not the largest, it certainly should be one of the largest. The sending church should also feel primarily responsible for the emergency, medical, and transportation needs of the missionary. While the sending church may not be able to bear this alone, the home pastor can lead his church to do as much as possible from within the congregation, and then he can assist by calling other churches to help as well.

Second, we must be willing to visit our missionaries. I have heard pastors complain against missions boards for telling a man that he should leave the field. At first, this complaint seemed legitimate. The problem in one case, however, was that the missionary had become immoral on the foreign field, and the local church pastor was unwilling to visit and intervene in the problem firsthand. When the missions agency sent a field representative to discuss this with the family, there was no question that the missionary needed to come home immediately. This was not the result of a "strong-arming missions board" but rather of an uninvolved home pastor.

If we are going to deputize men and women to go forth from our churches to the mission field, we must be involved in their lives after they go! This will mean visiting their fields from time to time for the purpose of edifying their families and involving ourselves in the work of ministries that have become extensions of our own local churches.

Third, we must nurture the family needs of a missionary. This may be done by remembering the missionary and family members on birthdays, anniversaries, and at special times of the year such as Christmas. The sending church should also occasionally send care packages and special love offerings simply to encourage and be a blessing.

The sending church should remember to nurture the missionary family spiritually. In today's high-tech society, this can be done by sending videos of recent church services or other special events. It will be immensely beneficial to send good Christian music, encouraging books, and other tools of spiritual encouragement throughout the year.

In some instances, missionaries do not seek out a relationship with the pastor, much like the behavior of some church members at home. As a general rule, however, a missionary should send a personal email at least once a month to the sending pastor. This email should involve a report regarding the spiritual lives of the missionary and his family, as well as the open-hearted sharing of spiritual struggles and critical prayer requests.

We have several missionaries sent forth from Lancaster Baptist Church. These missionaries regularly send personal emails to me, as their pastor, in order that I might pray more specifically for the needs of the missionary families. We maintain an open, encouraging, iron-sharpening-iron relationship that nurtures spiritual growth and health, even across the many miles.

Another area of practical help for the missionary family involves the children's education. We have sometimes provided a year of schooling tuition-free for missionaries' children while their parents are on furlough. If a church has a Christian school, I believe this should be a standard offering so that their children may acclimate to a good Christian culture while they are home and continue their quality academic development at the same time.

Besides the Christian school experience, a local church may help obtain teaching supplies, books and other needed materials to send to a missionary wife who may be home-schooling her children on the field.

We must help provide care for missionaries when they return home on furlough. Re-entry into American culture is very difficult after serving on a foreign field. Every sending church should make it a priority to nurture a missionary and his family through this time of readjustment. In addition, there are special financial considerations, living arrangements, transportation needs, and family education needs that a home church should consider and help to meet.

The Sending Church as a Reference

The sending church pastor should also do his best to be a reference for the missionary during deputation or furlough. He can be a tremendous blessing by sending letters or making phone calls to other pastors recommending a missionary.

In addition, the sending church should also help with the cost of prayer cards and brochures to promote the missionary who is sent from their church. This should not be the burden of the missionary alone, but should be shared with his church family. When the time of furlough arrives, the home pastor should consider helping to line up meetings, provide temporary lodging, assist with transportation needs, etc.

In short, in obedience to the leading of the Holy Spirit, a pastor and local church family must be sensitive to help the missionary family as they step out in obedience to the Lord. There is a great responsibility upon the sending church and its pastor, even as there is a responsibility on the missionary who is going to the foreign field.

Finally, when a church has a pastoral change, it should be clearly understood by the incoming pastor that there is a relationship and a responsibility to a family or several families on the mission field.

This new pastor should accept this relationship and do everything in his power to assure that the missionaries sent by that church will be honored and cared for as the Holy Spirit would have it.

May God help us follow the pattern of Acts 13 and 14 and be the sending agencies that He has intended us to be for His glory!

CHAPTER SIX

Deputation

Dwight Tomlinson

Rangoon, November 14, 1816

My beloved Rev. Luther Rice,

In encouraging other young men to come out as missionaries, do use the greatest caution. One wrong-headed, conscientiously obstinate fellow would ruin us. Humble, quiet, persevering men; men of sound, sterling talents, (though, perhaps, not brilliant), of decent accomplishments, and some natural aptitude to acquire a language; men of an amiable, yielding temper, willing to take the lowest place, to be the least of all and the servants of all; men who enjoy much closet religion, who live near to God, and are willing to suffer all things for Christ's sake, without being proud of it, these are the men. But O, how unlike to this description is the writer of it! Still, however, I am, with never-ceasing affection.

Your most affectionate brother in the Lord,
Adoniram Judson

Think about the words of one of the greatest servants of God who ever lived as you contemplate deputation. Adoniram Judson was the first missionary ever to leave the shores of America to sail to a distant land for the purpose of leading people to Christ and planting local New Testament churches.

When Adoniram Judson arrived in Burma in 1813, the Gospel of Jesus Christ had not touched even one Burmese soul. He spent the next thirty years enduring hardness, sickness, imprisonment, and personal tragedy while following God's commandment to preach the Gospel to every creature. He did not win even one soul to Christ during his first six years in the country, yet at the time of his death in 1850, sixty-three Burmese churches, and thousands of believers mourned his passing. On the one-hundredth anniversary of his death, there were approximately 200,000 Christians in Burma.

It is significant that Adoniram Judson's philosophy and approach to missions was very similar to what we see in many Baptist churches today. Independent Baptist churches still understand what he so succinctly stated in this letter nearly two hundred years ago. We must send our *best* to the mission field, and we must place Christ-like character above all other considerations.

Missionaries, themselves, are the best or worst advertisements for full-time missionary work, and in this chapter we will explore how and why to enter a season of deputation effectively.

What Is Deputation and Why Do It?

A *deputy* is one who acts on behalf of another; thus, the missionary is seeking churches who will deputize him—allow him to go on their behalf to places they cannot go. Deputation as we know it today is the act of the new missionary traveling from church to church presenting his burden and soliciting prayer and financial support from the various churches. Normally, he will do this until he has raised his target goal of financial support, at which time he will depart for the field. The process of deputation can happen in as little as a year or as many as three years depending upon several factors.

The process looks more difficult than it really is. That is not to minimize the very real challenges and difficulties. There is a price to pay for this method of raising missionary support. The price is paid in time and finances as well as in physical and emotional drain. Even though there is a price to pay, the dividends are great.

First, let me acknowledge that the exact manner in which independent Baptists normally handle deputation *today* is not spelled out in the Scriptures. That is not to say that deputation is not scriptural, for it most certainly is. The principle of local churches supporting missionaries is thoroughly biblical; the method of how that comes about is one that has developed as need and opportunity has arisen. As God has enlarged the opportunities that American churches have to evangelize the world, these same churches have used biblical commands and principles to streamline raising the financial support that enables a missionary family to live and work full-time on a foreign field.

We do not see Paul and his fellow missionaries traveling from church to church raising support before going to the countries the Holy Spirit directed them to. But we do see them being sent out and supported by a local church and other churches adding to the financial and prayer support of the first missionaries as time went by. An example of this would be Paul being supported at first by the church in Antioch, and later the church of Philippi, adding their support as Paul went to Thessalonica to start the church there. It is reasonable to suppose that the Thessalonican believers added their encouragement as Paul left them to go towards Corinth. In fact, Paul later stated that it was other churches (Antioch, Philippi, Thessalonica, etc.) that paid his salary as he started a church in the city of Corinth (2 Corinthians 11:8).

There is significant biblical evidence for this process of deputation—the act of multiple churches working together to provide the support for a missionary, and it is imperative for local churches to work together in supporting and praying for missionaries as they attempt to get to the field.

The Benefits of Deputation

Deputation has many benefits as the prospective missionary will be helped in his personal life and ministry by the deputation experience. What are these benefits?

1. Securing Financial Support

This is obviously a first goal of deputation. There is nothing innately unspiritual or selfish about having this goal. The missionary is attempting to raise both personal and work support, which will enable him to live and serve on the field full-time. The amount of financial support will differ from various fields. The missionary should consult with his missions agency to determine the amount needed.

2. Securing Prayer Support

Along with financial support, every Christian worker needs an undergirding of prayer support. The missionary is engaged in spiritual warfare that sometimes is more intense than it is at home. The forces of darkness may have held sway over the religious, political, and social life of the country for centuries or even millenniums. Satan and his demons will not easily give ground to seeing the kingdom of darkness penetrated with the light of God's truth. The missionaries need to be protected by a constant barrage of prayer from supporting churches at home.

3. Securing Co-laborers

There are others in local churches across America that God desires to call to the harvest fields of this world. Those laborers will be reached and discipled through the local church, and they will be burdened by the example of others who have heard and responded to the call.

We must never underestimate the power of example and the power of preaching during deputation. There is tremendous power in hearing a dedicated young man who has forsaken all to follow the Saviour as he takes the Word of God and pleads for others to join him. I have spoken to hundreds of missionaries, and virtually all of them will point to a camp, a missions conference, or some type of preaching service where God first burdened their hearts to serve as missionaries. They will often mention a visual presentation of the field as being one of the most compelling vehicles God used to burden them for a particular country or people group.

4. Securing the Edification of the Church

There is no place for selfishness in the local church. Deputation is a ministry, and it is an end in itself, as well as a means to an end. Deputation provides a tremendous opportunity for a visiting missionary to have a positive, encouraging influence upon a pastor and a local church family. A missionary must enter this time with a heart to serve, encourage, and edify each church he visits.

If the missionary goes to churches only to receive but not to give, he will harm the cause of Christ. Yes, he is hoping to receive the three things mentioned earlier—financial support, prayer support, and co-laborers—but deputation is also about giving.

The missionary must remember that he is there to *give* a blessing as well as to *receive* one. If the missionary will do his best to humbly serve the pastor and the church, he is sure to receive a blessing in return. He should not fear his ability to raise financial support. God always honors those that honor Him. He will always provide for those who attempt to unselfishly serve His people.

A church that has been edified by the biblical preaching and sacrificial example of guest missionaries will, in return, love and support those missionaries. Do not minimize this aspect of deputation. God desires to use this time to allow the missionary to share the vision, encourage the local churches, and edify the saints.

5. Securing Much Needed Ministry Experience

A young missionary candidate usually has more zeal than knowledge. This is not a criticism or an insult, but rather the natural result of a young life-calling that does not have much experience behind it. The only way to gain this needed experience is to immerse your life into ministry environments that will provide foundational growth and biblical understanding.

John Eliot, missionary to the Indians of Massachusetts, used to say: "Prayer and pains through faith in Jesus Christ will do anything." Prayer and pains are necessary ingredients in the life of God's servants. *Prayer* expresses our dependence upon God. *Pains* involve the daily enduring of ministry efforts and spiritual battle.

One of the great benefits of deputation is that a young missionary couple can learn the value of determination. Deputation is a natural "weeding process" so to speak. We do not need men on the field that are not willing to sacrifice to get there. If a person expects everything to be handed to him on a silver platter without work or effort, he will be very disappointed in the ministry and will lack the determination required to bear fruit that remains.

The process of deputation also exposes the missionary candidate to successful pastors and churches from whom he may learn and increase his own effectiveness. He will be exposed to both urban and rural churches as well as large and small ministries. This exposure will sharpen his own ability and build wisdom and discernment as a servant of God.

The ministry, sacrifice, and endurance required for deputation is a very important part of the maturing process of young missionaries.

Deputation: Getting Started

How does a young missionary get started on the deputation trail? I would suggest that you first make an appointment with your sending pastor. Allow him to approve the "right time" in your life to begin pursuing the mission field. There are many potential dangers and spiritual battles related to entering missions work, and you must rely upon the insight and experience of a godly pastor that you can trust. The pastor may suggest an internship, additional education, or perhaps a waiting time to prove the Holy Spirit's leading in your life. Allow the Holy Spirit to guide your local church in approving you for the work—do not rush this process. This is both wise and biblical.

Once you have your pastor's blessing, it is time to begin making concrete plans. You have finished your internship. Before you actually begin deputation, it is imperative that you take care of a few critical details. First, you should decide if you will partner with a missions agency or if you will strictly be sent from your local church. If you decide to go with a missions agency, this will involve counseling with your pastor, choosing the agency, and entering into the necessary process with that agency. Then you should prepare your media materials for deputation. This involves designing and printing your prayer card and perhaps a brochure stating your testimony, your purpose, and your vision for your work abroad. It will also involve the preparation of a brief video presentation introducing your family, your calling, and your field. Your materials should also include some references from your home pastor and church. With these details in place, you are ready to begin the actual process of securing the necessary funds to live and work on the field.

One of the things you and your sending pastor should discuss is the length of time you plan to spend on deputation. I would suggest that you prayerfully set a time limit for leaving America and going to the field. A target date as well as a monetary target will give you the impetus to keep on working when you feel like slowing down. It will be a constant reminder that you have a job to do and you must stay focused and work hard to reach your goal of getting to the field by a certain date. The goal should be reasonable, yet it should require faith to attain.

The missionary on deputation should attempt to be in a minimum of two churches every week and to *attend* no less than three services per week. The churches you are visiting and the pastors you are asking for money will usually be accustomed to having church services three times a week along with their busy work schedules. With a little advance planning, missionaries will be able to be in three churches a week without much difficulty. Your goal is to have prearranged meetings where the pastor will allow you to present your burden for the field. Yet, even if you are not speaking or officially representing your missions efforts, you should be in church regardless. If for some reason you find yourself with a free service on a church night, attend a service nearby and introduce yourself to the pastor. You never know if your presence in that service might generate a future invitation to present your ministry. Even if that is not the case, God will bless your faithfulness to His priorities.

How to Get Meetings

1. A Letter of Introduction

If you are just getting started as an unknown missionary, your sending pastor should send out a letter of introduction on your behalf. It is important for you to realize that your sending pastor is not responsible for raising your support. It is not his job to get on the phone and secure your meetings, and it is wrong for you to expect him to do so. It is not unreasonable to ask him to send out a letter of recommendation as your sending pastor. This letter should go out to all of the churches in the geographical area in which you hope to raise your support. Obviously, it is preferable to raise your support within one or two regions of the country. This will make the most of your travel time and budget, and it will also serve to help in reporting back to your supporting churches when you return from the field on furlough.

2. Follow Up with Personal Phone Calls

Once the letter has been sent, it is imperative that you follow up each letter with a personal call. Most pastors are not going to call you to invite you to speak. This is not due to their lack of concern, but to their busy schedules and the assumption that you will call them. Add to this the fact that you are not the only one calling, and you will realize that you must take the initiative to generate the contact. This will be your first chance to prove the sincerity and intensity of your burden. You will have to make many calls to keep your schedule full, and many smaller churches do not have staff to answer phones. Be prepared to be diligent. You must not allow discouragement to keep you from staying on the phone to book future meetings.

When you do contact a person at a church, ask to speak to the pastor. Be honest about who you are and the nature of your call. Do not deceive the receptionist by being deliberately vague. It may mean that occasionally a receptionist will cut you off and tell you that the church is not taking on any more missionaries at the present, but it is not your place to lie about why you are calling in hopes of being able to pressure the pastor into a meeting. I agree that a receptionist should not tell you that your ministry will not be considered, but it is going to happen. Just accept this fact and predetermine ahead of time not to get upset about it.

Once you get through to the pastor, tell him who you are, what church you are from, and ask him if it would be possible to come by and present your burden for the foreign field. If he is not able to have you at that time, be polite and understanding. Remember that the whole world does not revolve around you and your calling. God already has the churches He knows will partner with you, and your job is to stay on the phone until you find them.

3. Make Calls from Church Directories

It is probably not possible or desirable to raise your support strictly from the churches contacted by your pastor. God probably has a wider circle of influence for you than you could possibly imagine. There are churches that need you just as much as you need them! You are not a *beggar*; you are an *ambassador*, according to 2 Corinthians 5:20. Do not be ashamed to call pastors whom you do not know. The vast majority of them are men of God with a heart to reach the world with the Gospel. It has been almost twenty-five years since I started on the deputation trail, and to this day, some of my dearest friends are pastors I met as a result of cold calls from a directory of independent Baptist churches while on deputation.

4. Attend Preacher's Meetings if You Are Able

If you can arrange to be in an area when a large meeting of pastors is taking place, it will be worthwhile to attend. This should not be done if you have to spend a great deal of money to get there or if you do not have any meetings in the area. But if you are able to schedule some local church meetings in the area, and it would not require you to compromise your beliefs to attend a particular meeting, then do it. Remember to let God guide you. Do not make a nuisance of yourself. It is not necessary to hand every pastor a prayer card or hit them up for a meeting in the restroom! Your purpose is to get your name out, meet some people, and let God guide you to the men that He has already chosen to partner with you.

In conclusion, let me reiterate that there are many benefits to deputation. Someone has rightly said that your attitude at the beginning of a task will determine its success. Go into deputation with a positive attitude, excited and surrendered to the will of God, and you will find it to be a rich and rewarding experience.

CHAPTER SEVEN

Your Supporting Churches

Dwight Tomlinson

We have seen that the New Testament gives us the plan of multiple churches providing financial support for a missionary, as opposed to one church assuming the entire responsibility for his care. The church at Antioch in Acts 13 was the original "sending church," when they obeyed the Holy Spirit and sent Barnabas and Saul out for the work which they had been called. It can be assumed that they initially took responsibility for the entire care of the two missionaries. However, by the second missionary journey, there were other churches helping to finance the missionary work. For example, Paul did not receive a salary from the church at Corinth during the time that he was their pastor. It was his desire to not hinder the introduction of the Gospel message in that city by appearing to be preaching for the purpose of financial gain. He wanted to remove this area of potential criticism.

How then was Paul supported? There were two means that God used to meet Paul's needs as he founded the Corinthian church. He engaged in the trade of tent-making, which afforded him finances to stay in Corinth, and he was supported financially by the missions offerings of other churches. Later, when writing about this to the church at Corinth, he made the statement that he *"robbed other churches"* (2 Corinthians 11:8). Notice he was supported by *churches*, plural, which tells us that it was not just the church at Antioch sending missions offerings to Paul while he was in Corinth.

The same thing was true when Paul and his missionary team started the church in the city of Thessalonica. There were other churches besides Antioch sending offerings to help the team devote themselves full-time to the work of church planting. The New Testament book of Philippians is a letter written to the church at Philippi thanking them for the offerings they sent to the Apostle Paul during his second missionary journey (Philippians 4:14–18).

The book of Acts teaches that the churches who started supporting Paul on the first missionary journey were involved in helping Paul with both finances and manpower on the second and third missionary journeys. Those young churches provided both offerings and people to continue the furtherance of the Gospel. They understood from the beginning that they had a responsibility to not only receive the Gospel, but to also send it!

This privilege of mission churches reproducing themselves by supporting missionaries is at the heart of church planting. Missionary pastors must instill a vision of supporting missions in every new church they start. Around the world today there are churches sending out missionaries from places that were considered mission fields themselves just a few years ago! I started the Bible Baptist Church of Kowloon in Hong Kong, China, in 1984. A few years later, they commissioned and sent me to start the Bay Area Baptist Church in Newark, California. Today, both The Bible Baptist Church and the Bay Area Baptist Church are supporting missions. That is God's plan. We are blessed to be a blessing, not simply to be blessed. As every church was at one time a mission church, today every church should be involved in planting new churches, both at home and abroad through the support of missions.

In this chapter we will consider two aspects of supporting-churches. First, we will study the responsibility of the missionary to the supporting-church, and second, we will study the responsibility of the supporting-church to the missionary.

The Responsibility of the Missionary to the Host Church

1. Tell the Truth

It is imperative that a missionary, called of God to leave home and take the message of Jesus Christ to a foreign land, be a person of absolute integrity. If you are prone to lies, exaggerations, and gossip, you should stay home until you have dealt with these basic character issues. You owe it to your supporting churches to be a person of integrity! That means that when you preach, you tell the truth about the condition and need of your field. It is not necessary to embellish the truth by making your field sound needier or more difficult than it is in reality. Some missionaries, for instance, make statements that there are absolutely no churches in the city to which they are going. If that is the case, it is proper to say it. But, if what they really mean is that there are no churches identified directly with their missions board, but there are other independent Baptist groups with thriving works, they should state it accurately.

There are places that have absolutely no Gospel-preaching churches, and if that is the case, by all means someone needs to lay the burden on God's people to get the Gospel there as quickly as possible. Simply put, every pastor and church family should be able to fully trust what a missionary states from their pulpit.

2. *Never Go behind the Pastor's Back to Solicit Funds*

The pastor has been given the responsibility to watch over the flock as the under-shepherd. There are several New Testament words that describe the one office of a pastor. He is called bishop, elder, and pastor in the New Testament. These three titles are used interchangeably, each one describing a different function of his office.

The word *bishop* means overseer. It is the pastor's responsibility to oversee every aspect of the church ministry. That includes missions support. It is highly unethical for a missionary to usurp God's structure to solicit funds from individual church members without the pastor's knowledge and consent. I believe it is unethical for a missionary to send his prayer letter to the individual members of the church unless they are his immediate relatives, or unless there are unusual circumstances to which the pastor has agreed.

A missionary may be in a church on deputation and a family takes a particular interest in him for one reason or another. That family may even request to be on the missionary's mailing list. I think the wise missionary would gently and kindly explain that it is his policy to mail the letter to the church body as a whole through the pastor, and that he would be uncomfortable mailing it to individual members. This should be explained kindly so as to not be offensive to the church member. It should also be very clearly stated that it is the missionary's policy, not the requirement of the pastor.

Most pastors receive solicitations for donations on a daily basis, and they should have the liberty to prayerfully consider which, if any, of the needs are brought before the church. It is not right for a missionary to take that matter into his own hands by soliciting funds without the pastor's knowledge.

On occasion I have heard of unethical missionaries deliberately seeking out individuals in a church body that have more financial means for the express purpose of soliciting individual support.

God will not bless this sort of underhanded approach to ministry. Be ethical, honest, and above-board in all your communications. Submit yourself to God's structure of authority within each local church—namely the pastor and his philosophy of ministry. In doing so, you are guaranteeing that God will bless you and your work in a greater way.

Finally, on this point, if a church member approaches you personally about private support, you should kindly defer that giving and encourage it back to and through the local church. Encourage that church member to take their burden to the pastor and to perhaps designate it towards missions through their regular giving in their church. It would also be advisable to mention that particular situation to the pastor to protect your own integrity as a missionary.

3. Be a Servant and an Example While You Are a Guest of the Church

Never forget that your calling is to serve and not to be served. If you set out to serve God's people asking nothing in return, God will make sure that you are richly rewarded. The principle of sowing and reaping will be very evident in your life and ministry if you trust God and seek to be a blessing. Certainly there will be some churches that take advantage of you, but they will be in the vast minority, and God will make sure that you are treated better at the next church!

Your attitude needs to be one of gratitude and willingness to render humble service for the glory of God. If you go into the churches with a humble servant's attitude, you will find the vast majority of churches will be extremely kind to you.

While you are visiting a church, whether on deputation or on furlough, participate in ministry. Attend soulwinning challenges and find opportunities to win people to Christ and see them come to church and be baptized. Do the work of missions whether you are on your field or not. What better way to show a pastor your true heart than to win souls to Christ and find new prospects while you are visiting! As a pastor, I would find it very difficult to refuse support to this kind of missionary!

Look for other opportunities to serve and to get involved. Be a blessing in construction projects, workdays, and other ministry projects when possible. Ask the pastor what you can do or how you can help. In doing so, you will hold forth an excellent example of a true servant and ambassador of Christ.

4. Be Careful to Stay within the Allotted Time, if You Are Given an Opportunity to Preach or Teach

There are many factors—of which you may not be aware—that could necessitate the pastor asking you to be finished by a certain time. There are probably multiple services going on at the same time which need to be coordinated with the children's services. For instance, in the church which I pastor in Southern California, our services are being conducted in English, Chinese, and Spanish simultaneously. It is important that we all finish relatively close to the same time in order for the nurseries and children's ministries to plan their programs.

It would be arrogant for a guest speaker to assume that he did not need to abide by the accepted norms set by the pastor. If the congregation is accustomed to being dismissed by noon, and the visiting missionary preaches until 1:00 PM, that missionary will probably find himself not being added to the support list of that particular church. That is especially true if the pastor asked him to be finished by 12:00! Before you claim that spiritual people ought not to be concerned about time when it comes to the preaching of God's Word, stop and remember that the mind can only receive what the seat can endure! The problem is probably not the lack of spirituality of the listener, but the lack of ability of the speaker. Stay within the allotted time and be thankful for whatever opportunity you have to present your field.

At the heart, this shows a basic, appropriate respect for the pastor and the church family. It shows a servant's heart and a submissive spirit.

5. *Stay Focused on the Subject of Missions*

If the pastor asks you to speak on another subject, then by all means do your best to honor his request. Otherwise, stay focused on missions. There may be some occasions where the Holy Spirit will lead you to preach on a different topic than missions, but as a general rule, a missionary on deputation will attempt to burden the church for the people to whom God has called him. After all, that is why you are there in the first place. You were invited to present the needs of your field and teach the people their responsibility and privilege in fulfilling the Great Commission.

There are two things that should happen as a result of your being in the services that day. First, the people should be able to sense your burden and love for the people you are called to reach. Second, the missions giving should increase, or at least the people should be more inclined to give. If a missionary comes into a church with a passion for souls and a servant's heart, the Holy Spirit will use that example to compel God's people to give more faithfully and in a greater way! There is not a lack of missions money in America; there is a lack of motivation to give it. No one wants to give money to a project they do not deem worthy, but if they really sense the need, they will give generously. Americans are the most generous people on earth, but they must believe that they are giving to something that will really make a difference.

Another reason to stay focused on the subject of missions is that you want to be a help and not a hindrance to the pastor. The pastor has been called to give direction to the church in sensitive areas, not the visiting missionary. You may see some things that in your opinion should be straightened out, but remember that it is not your place to deal with issues. Your attempt to "fix" a problem might leave the pastor with a much bigger problem than he had before you fixed it!

6. Do not Lose Sight of the Big Picture

Never forget that you are on a divine mission. You have been called of God to take the Gospel to a people that are dying in spiritual darkness, waiting for you to bring them the light. Every day you delay is another day they wait. How many people will die and go to Hell while you carelessly flitter away precious time and resources?

The work you are called to is the most important in all of the world, and it deserves to be treated as such. You are an ambassador, not a travel agent. Nor are you on an extended vacation, spending several years touring America at the churches' expense! You are there to raise prayer and financial support so you can get quickly to the field and win souls. Work hard at getting meetings and laying a burden on hearts for your field. Take the advice of William Carey, another great missionary whose steps you should follow, "Work as if everything depended upon you, and pray as if everything depended upon God."

The Responsibility of the Host Church to the Missionary

1. Be Honest with the Missionary Concerning Support

Pastor, the young couple coming to your church was honest with you about why they wanted to come. They asked if they could come and present their work. You knew exactly what that meant when you allowed them to come. You know that the missionary candidate is not coming because he needs practice in the fine art of preaching. Although he may very well need practice, that is not why he is there. He is there with the same hope of which missionary, Paul, spoke in 2 Corinthians 10:15–16 when he said *"...having hope, when your faith is increased, that we shall be enlarged by you according to our rule abundantly, to preach the gospel in the regions beyond you...."*

The missionary's hope is that your church will be burdened to step out by faith and help him with a monthly financial commitment so he can get his family to the field and begin winning souls and planting churches.

If a pastor knows in advance that he will not be adding new missionaries in the foreseeable future, he should tell the missionary up front before scheduling the meeting. When I was raising support to go to the field of Hong Kong, China, I sometimes had pastors tell me that they were not in a position to take on new missionaries, but they would like to have me come and help them burden their people for missions. I always gladly accepted those meetings and appreciated the integrity that the pastor showed in being truthful with me about the possibility of support. I knew going into the meeting that we were not likely to raise monthly support, but that I had the opportunity to help the pastor in whatever way he desired. In many of those cases, the church did eventually begin supporting us financially. Yet, with or without support, I rejoiced in the privilege of presenting our burden and trying to be a blessing to the faithful and honest pastor.

There were a few cases, however, where I showed up at a church only to find that I was being used as pulpit supply while the pastor was on vacation. It was disappointing in those situations to discover there would be no consideration of support. I believe it is unethical to use a missionary in such a way without letting him know in advance.

I am not against using a missionary to cover the pulpit in the pastor's absence. In fact, I recently scheduled a vacation with my wife and children and booked a missionary to preach in my place. This particular missionary has been a personal friend for over twenty years and has been supported by our church for over fifteen years. Our people know and love him, and he knew in advance that I would not be here on the Sunday that he was to preach. Having a trusted friend like him can be a great help to the church and a relief to the pastor.

2. Tell the Missionary Candidate Up Front What Your Expectations Are

These missionaries are traveling across America trying to raise the financial support needed to get to the field. They will probably be in hundreds of different churches before they get to the field. Every one of those churches will be different in some aspect, and some of them will be *very* different!

If you only support missionaries who attended a particular school, identify with a particular movement within fundamentalism, use a particular style of preaching, or eat a certain style of food, that is your prerogative; but you should make that clear before the missionary arrives at your church.

For example, our church feels very strongly about the King James version of the Bible. We do not expect the missionary to use it in a country that does not speak English, but if he is preaching in our church to our English congregation (we currently have both a Spanish and a Chinese department as a part of our church) I expect him to preach from a King James Bible. If a missionary came to the church that I pastor and preached from another Bible version, he would not be likely to leave with a commitment from us for monthly financial support.

I believe it is my responsibility, not the missionaries', to make sure that we only invite like-minded missionaries to present their work to our church family. Therefore, I am careful who I allow in our pulpit. For instance, we decided long ago, as a church, that we would only support missionaries that are clear in their stand on the Baptist distinctives, and we make sure this is known to any prospective missionary before a meeting is scheduled.

I am not advocating that we invite people to preach who are merely going to parrot back to us what they think we want to hear. My point is Liberty Baptist Church is a Baptist church with a limited amount of missions resources given by Baptist people for the support of Baptist missionaries. As the pastor, I have an obligation to be a good steward of those gifts and to carefully select potential missionaries for support.

So what is a pastor to do? Should he drill every missionary who calls for a meeting on his doctrinal stand? A pastor could do that, but there is an easier way. I simply ask a few basic questions such as where he went to school, which missions board he is using, and who is his sending church. The answer to those three questions will tell me immediately if I want to question him a little further for clarification. By the way, I am not going to make a decision based solely upon a particular school or missions board. The answer to these questions might simply prompt me to dig a little deeper as to his personal beliefs. The issue that should be considered is what the man believes and practices, not whether I recommend the school he attended!

3. Let Him Know How Long You Want Him to Preach or Teach

If he is teaching a class and the class needs to be dismissed at a certain time, tell him. Do not feel bad about giving time restraints and clear instructions. Most missionaries will appreciate this.

4. Give Him a Reasonable Love Offering to Meet the Needs of He and His Family

I understand all churches are in different stages as to what they are able to do financially, but every church should do their best to make sure that the missionary's needs are met. With minimal advance planning you could be sure that there is someone to sign the love offering check, or better yet, predetermine a generous love offering from your missions budget and have the check prepared before the meeting. Do not tell the missionary, "the check is in the mail," especially when we know that most pastors who say that can not seem to locate the post office! If you tell a missionary that you are going to send a check, then by all means keep your word.

Consider this, the missionary you are hosting may very well need your love offering to buy gas to make it to his next meeting. He may have children with medical needs, and he most definitely will need the money to feed his family and stay on the road during deputation.

5. Be Considerate about Accommodations for the Missionary and His Family

He is a servant and does not need to be put up in the Taj Mahal, but he also should not be expected to sleep on a sleeping bag in an old Sunday school room that is infested with mice, cockroaches, and mold. The golden rule would apply here. Put him somewhere that you would not mind staying yourself. Place his family in a place that you would lodge your own family. It is not always necessary to place him in a hotel if you have a good family with a nice clean place to host a guest.

I was once placed with a young couple in Washington State in the dead of winter. I was traveling alone for this particular meeting. The husband informed me that he would be leaving at 5:30 in the morning for work, but I should sleep in and his wife would cook me breakfast whenever I woke up. Obviously, I had no choice but to leave the house at 5:30 in the morning when he did. There was no way I was going to be at home alone with his wife while he was at work! I got up the next morning, left at 5:30, and went to Denny's where I drank coffee and waited for the sun to come up. All the while, I read my Bible and thought good thoughts about the pastor that put me in such a questionable position.

6. If You Promise Monthly Support, Be True to Your Word and Send the Funds

It is dishonest to tell a missionary that you are going to support him and then not follow through. Pastors should not trust their memory on this. I have occasionally made a commitment to a missionary only to completely forget that I did. Only later did I remember my mistake and make it right. Another time I made a commitment to a church planter on the East Coast. A full year transpired without his acknowledging receipt of our checks. When I questioned him as to his not writing, he informed me that he had never received our checks! The problem turned out to be a computer error by our office. We had placed the support on a memorized transaction setting that is designed to automatically print checks each month. The problem was that we failed to check the box that instructed the printer to print the check. As a result, we generated a monthly statement showing that the check had been printed and sent when in reality it had not been. As soon as we figured out the problem, we wrote him a check for the entire year's support on the spot.

I always ask missionaries to write and remind me if we make a commitment of support. I have learned through the years not to trust my memory.

7. Consider Supporting Fewer Missionaries at Larger Amounts

The average independent Baptist missionary now spends in excess of two years raising support. He must visit hundreds of churches and travel thousands of miles, while spending tens of thousands of dollars to sustain his family on the road. I think it is time for our churches to at least consider increasing support levels as a means of wise stewardship of the finances with which God has entrusted us.

When I went to the field in 1983, the average church support was $50.00 per month. The missionaries I talk with today tell me it is currently between $75.00 and $100.00. Let us suppose that a missionary needed to raise $5,000.00 per month in support to go to his particular field. Some countries would require more, and some less, but let us use the figure of $5,000.00 for illustration sake. If the average support is $50.00, the missionary must enlist 100 supporting churches, which means he would need to preach in 200 churches, if he secured support from one half of the churches. If the average support was $100.00, he would only need to present his ministry in 100 churches. I believe we should seriously consider an average support level of $200.00 per month. That would mean the missionary would only need to present his work in 50 churches and pick up 25 of them, which could easily be done in less than a year. This would save multiplied thousands of dollars of God's money to be used for the actual planting of churches on the foreign field.

I realize that not all churches are able, nor do they desire, to support missionaries at $200.00 per month. I am not advocating a certain dollar amount as much as I am encouraging a pastor to re-think the support issue, and then do whatever he believes God is leading him to do.

One argument for a missionary having more churches at smaller amounts is that he then has a larger support base for prayer and special needs. Another argument for smaller amounts is that if the missionary loses a supporting church for some reason, it will not hurt him as much. These are both valid reasons to have more supporting churches at smaller amounts, but if the average amount were raised to $150.00 or $200.00, the missionary would still have a large enough support base and not be devastated if he did lose a church for some reason.

In conclusion, let me just reiterate that we are in this work as co-laborers. It is the greatest task in which we can engage, and it is worthy of our prayerful planning and consideration. Missionaries and supporting churches are on the same team. If we will consider each other and prefer each other in love, we will accomplish great things for the cause of Christ together.

PART THREE

Getting Settled on the Field

CHAPTER EIGHT

Arrival and Initial Ministry

Dwight Tomlinson

We left San Francisco on a Monday morning and flew sixteen hours via Taipei before finally arriving in Hong Kong on Wednesday evening. The plane landed at the Kai Tak airport where we passed through immigration, collected our luggage, and then cleared customs. I will never forget walking through the sliding glass doors that separated us from a large chaotic waiting room. The first sensation was the heat and humidity that felt as if it slapped you into a reality check in case you did not know that you had actually arrived on the southern tip of China. Next was the unfamiliar sound of hundreds of people speaking a seemingly unintelligible language. I remember the feeling of aloneness as we walked down the ramp into a sea of faces, none of which I recognized.

There we were in a strange land, not knowing the language, culture, or customs. Suddenly, out of the hundreds of people milling around I spotted my friend and the man who would be my co-worker! The feeling of relief was overwhelming when I realized I was not without a friend to help me in a strange country.

I wonder if the Apostle Paul felt the same when he moved to the city of Corinth to plant a church. He was in a strange city without a friend. Paul had left his companions in Thessalonica while he went alone to Athens and then to Corinth. Corinth was a large sea port city known for its immorality and vice, but God providentially provided a couple to come alongside Paul and help him establish a church for God's honor and glory. When God finds a missionary who will go to a city and carve out a work by faith, He will bring others into that missionary's life to help establish the church!

Acts 18 records the establishing of the church at Corinth. There are principles preserved in this chapter that will give us insight into church planting in the twenty-first century.

Arrival and Getting Settled

After these things Paul departed from Athens, and came to Corinth; And found a certain Jew named Aquila, born in Pontus, lately come from Italy, with his wife Priscilla; (because that Claudius had commanded all Jews to depart from Rome:) and came unto them. And because he was of the same craft, he abode with them, and wrought: for by their occupation they were tentmakers.—ACTS 18: 1–3

The first thing a new missionary must do after arriving on his field is to get settled with housing and the practical things of everyday life. Often there will be other missionaries that can help the new family by meeting them at the airport, arranging a place to stay, and helping them through the initial confusion of life in a strange land.

This seems to be what God provided for the Apostle Paul when he arrived in the city of Corinth. The Bible does not say how Paul "found" Aquila and Priscilla, just that he did. I have no doubt but that it was by divine appointment that these two were in Corinth and came into contact with Paul. Not only did they open their home to Paul, but their home eventually became the first meeting place for the new church.

God had sent them before Paul, preparing all of the pieces of the puzzle. God is in the church planting business, and He has cities all over the world that He is preparing for the Gospel. They are waiting for the soulwinning missionary to leave his comfort zone and step out by faith to follow God to the unreached areas of the globe. When the missionary arrives he will find that God has gone before Him, preparing the way!

In many cases it will be possible for the new missionary to make a trip to his field a few weeks or months prior to actually moving his family. If possible, it would be wise for both the husband and wife to make this survey trip together prior to the big move. The purpose of this trip is to prepare the way before the family arrives. This is the time to check on housing, schooling, bringing specific items, and all of the details that need to be settled before the move.

Banking and financial policies of the host country need to be understood. What are the visa requirements? Do we need to ship things over from the States, or can they be easily acquired in our new home? What type of power is used? Should we bring electrical appliances or not? Is the water safe to drink? Do we need to bring a water purifier and if so, what type? Where will we live? What language schools are available, if any? These and many other questions need to be answered on this survey trip if possible.

If a survey trip is not practical, there needs to be some other way of getting the answers to these questions. It can be done by telephone with missionaries already on the field or through email or internet research.

Above all of this, the most important thing to remember is that God is in control. Just as He prepared the way for Paul, so He is preparing the way for you! Do everything you can to plan and prepare for your arrival, but at some point, you just have to go and trust God that Aquila and Priscilla will be there to meet you!

When my family moved to Hong Kong in 1984, we had a Chinese friend who met us and stayed with us for the first two weeks. He was an incredible help in learning the transportation system, finding housing and other details, but I soon found out that God had been at work long before I arrived, bringing all the pieces together for the establishment of a great church that is still winning souls more than two decades later.

Initial Ministry

When you arrive on a foreign field, you don't speak the language, and you don't know the culture. Where does ministry begin? A faithful missionary serving on the field of Cambodia recently shared these insightful thoughts:

"Many people suffer kind of an identity crisis in that first year or two on foreign soil. You feel like a fifth-wheel. You can't speak the language, which means not only can you *not* lead people to Christ, but you also can't understand any of the preaching. (Of course, I am referring only to non-English speaking countries.) That opening time on the field can bring a lot of discouragement and cause you to ask yourself, 'Where do I fit in? What can I do for God during this time? Is it really that important for me to insist my wife and small children go to every service?' I know these don't sound like very spiritual questions for a man of God, but these are the realities of the early days on a field that speaks a foreign language. I have observed many families struggling to find where they really fit in both ministry and in their daily schedule. I have never heard these issues addressed in a class, nor read them in a book."

While many of these issues will be addressed when we talk about culture shock, I want to forewarn you that your first year will bring with it many unique challenges and potential discouragements. My greatest challenge to you regarding your initial ministry is that you patiently stay focused on the will of God, the learning of a new culture, and the planting of a local New Testament church. Though you cannot speak the language, you can pray, serve, smile, and honor the Lord. Even the love of Christ in your attitude and demeanor at church and around ministry circumstances can be used of God to make a difference. Rather than lament what you cannot do, immerse yourself joyfully in what you *can* do to honor the Lord, even through your limitations!

Remember that the work of the Holy Spirit is not bound by cultural or language barriers. The Holy Spirit can use you during these early days. Don't let the devil rob the joy of ministry through these initial times of testing.

As you begin ministry, it is important that you stay focused on soulwinning and church planting, and it is vital that you not become too focused on "doing ministry" the way it was done "back home." Notice the example of the Apostle Paul:

> *And he reasoned in the synagogue every sabbath, and persuaded the Jews and the Greeks. And when Silas and Timotheus were come from Macedonia, Paul was pressed in the spirit, and testified to the Jews that Jesus was Christ. And when they opposed themselves, and blasphemed, he shook his raiment, and said unto them, Your blood be upon your own heads; I am clean: from henceforth I will go unto the Gentiles. And he departed thence, and entered into a certain man's house, named Justus, one that worshipped God, whose house joined hard to the synagogue. And Crispus, the chief ruler of the synagogue, believed on the Lord with all his house; and many of the Corinthians hearing believed, and were baptized.—ACTS 18:4–8*

Once Paul was settled in his housing and tent-making profession, he got about the business for which he had come to Corinth in the first place. He had not come to Corinth to start a tent-making business, but to win souls and establish a church! It is my conviction that all missions ministry should have at its heart the winning of souls and planting of local New Testament churches. I understand support ministries, and they are a vital part of changing the world, but they are called "support" ministries for a reason. Medical missions, for instance, are not an end in themselves. Medical missions should have at their core treating the physical as a means of caring for the sin-sick soul. Jesus taught that if a man could gain all the world has to offer in physical and financial care, yet died and went to Hell, that man had gained nothing (Mark 8:36)!

I do believe that it is necessary to take a comprehensive view of the world, and I understand that there are many countries where traditional missionaries are not allowed entrance. The largest country in the world is Communist China, and as of this writing, foreigners are denied entrances if they seek to enter as traditional church-planting missionaries. God is not limited, however, by the decrees of government. He is the one that allows government to exist at all. Some of God's choicest servants are even now working in that vast country for the propagation of the faith and the planting of churches. How are they doing it? Through support ministries that are bringing them into contact with people who are hungry to know the true and living God.

Muslim countries are another example of places that are extremely hostile to the Gospel. It is not possible for missionaries to enter most of these countries in conventional ways. But God is able to open doors for those with the faith to go forward! We must simply remember for what purpose He opens the doors. He opens those doors so we can sow the seeds of the Gospel and so lost souls can come to Christ.

A restricted-access country will have to be entered through some type of service visa—teaching English, language study, business consultant, etc. We must find an itch and scratch it. In those situations, it is especially important that the Christian worker be sensitive to the leading of the Holy Spirit in his work. This is always important of course, but the reality is that a servant of God that is not Spirit filled and led can do tremendous damage to the cause of Christ in a limited-access country. He must realize that the cultural norms back home are not the same as his new field. Openly witnessing of Christ could cause him to be immediately expelled from the country and could result in harsh reprisal to innocent people.

That is not to say that he should not witness, for that is his purpose in entering the country. He should, however, follow our Lord's admonition to be as wise as serpents and as harmless as doves.

> Behold, I send you forth as sheep in the midst of
> wolves: be ye therefore wise as serpents, and harmless
> as doves.—MATTHEW 10:16

We sometimes elevate our culturally accepted ways of doing things to a position of biblical authority. For example, in America it is quite common and effective to have regularly scheduled soulwinning and visitation times, such as Tuesday evening or Saturday morning. We will use Acts 1:8 as a verse to teach our people that they should attend one or more of these times.

> But ye shall receive power, after that the Holy Ghost
> is come upon you: and ye shall be witnesses unto me
> both in Jerusalem, and in all Judaea, and in Samaria,
> and unto the uttermost part of the earth.—ACTS 1:8

There is absolutely nothing wrong with having regularly scheduled times to go witnessing, but is that what Acts 1:8 says?

No it does not. It does not say that we will "**do**" witnessing; it says that we will "**be**" witnesses! Let me state again that I am for having regularly scheduled soulwinning times, and our church has them. We must be careful though that we do not elevate our traditional practices to a point of scriptural authority.

Another area that we must be willing to reconsider is the area of when and where public services are conducted. I have preached many times in China and almost never in the same place twice. The services are moved from place to place, and the times are altered so as not to attract undue attention. This is not necessary in America, but it is in some countries. The missionary must stay focused on his purpose of winning souls and planting churches and not get sidetracked by the methodology "back home."

In chapter twelve we will address specific steps to take in church planting, but for now I wanted to give you these simple thoughts to consider concerning arrival and initial ministry. Let me conclude this chapter with an actual letter that I received recently from a young couple ministering in a limited-access nation. The only thing I am omitting is the name of the missionary and the name of the country in which they serve. Other than that, the letter is exactly as I received it. As you read this letter, think of the pressure that this family lives under each day. Think also how ludicrous it would be to expect them to conduct their ministry exactly as we do in the States.

> Dear praying partners,
>
> We are privileged to be your praying partners and co-laborers to reach the world for Christ.
>
> Just a note of reminder. We are serving in a place that is closed to foreign gospel ministers. In order for us to stay here as long as we can without being thrown out, we ask that you help us.
>
> It was reported by a Christian friend here that a package sent from the States was opened for inspection. I believe we

are watched closely. For our safety and for the Lord's work sake, please do not expose our identity unnecessarily.

As a reminder:

Please do not use Rev., Pastor, Evangelist, Missionary, Church, Bible or Christian etc. on the envelope. Use only Mr. or Mrs. if writing to my wife or I. Do not use a church envelope; use a blank one instead.

Do not post our letter, name, family pictures or area of ministry on your website. With the powerful internet search engine, our identity can be exposed easily if our information is posted on your website.

To God be the glory,
Brother and Mrs. _____

CHAPTER NINE

Missionary Relationships

Dwight Tomlinson

One of the most important aspects of world evangelization involves the ability of God's servants to get along with each other and work together for the greater good. This is not always easy. We should not be surprised that relational conflicts arise among missionaries. Why should they be spared the heartaches that plague their counterparts in the pastoral ministry? Pastors often do not get along, even when those pastors are a part of the same fellowship or association of independent Baptists. This inability to get along can be manifested by anything from indifference to outright hostility. This is not unique to our generation. God's men have always had conflicts. Abraham and Lot were brethren, yet they parted company. Paul and Barnabas both loved the Lord and the souls of men, yet the contention between them was so sharp that they went their separate ways.

It is unrealistic to believe that all missionaries are going to work in close harmony, yet even brethren that divide can do so without being divisive. It is not necessary to attack each other just because we do not feel at liberty to work in close relationship, sharing resources and ministry. The Bible is clear that there must be agreement on essentials if we are to walk and work together. I am afraid that oftentimes we are not divided by scriptural principles but by personal insecurities and prejudice. To the extent that our differences are not biblical but petty, we must attempt, by the grace of God, to die to self and work in harmony. Much damage has been done to the cause of Christ by the pettiness of preachers.

Let us consider God's plan and desire for His servants to work together in mutual love and respect with others of like mind and purpose (Ephesians 4:1–3).

The early church sent missionaries out in teams. The first missionaries went out from the church in Antioch. The team consisted of Barnabas and Saul, later called Paul. Then Paul and Silas went out together on a church planting, missionary journey. Barnabas and John Mark went out together. Paul always had team members with whom he worked. He traveled with Luke, Silas, Timothy, Titus, and others as he planted churches in first century Asia.

Where did the early church get the concept of team missions? They learned it from Jesus Christ Himself who founded the church by sending His disciples out two by two, not one by one (Mark 6:7). There are many practical reasons for doing this. Missionary teams can encourage each other and pool resources and knowledge. Two are better than one, the Scripture tells us in the book of Ecclesiastes. This certainly applies in missions. By this, I do not necessarily mean that two missionary families should go out together, raising support and moving to the field at the same time, although there is certainly nothing wrong with that. What I mean is that missionaries should be willing to learn from and encourage each other in the work. We need to see ourselves as co-laborers, not competitors.

Most countries to which a new missionary goes will already have at least one like-minded missionary family there. It makes sense for the missionaries to at least meet together with some type of regularity for prayer, encouragement, and biblical fellowship. That may not be possible because of distance, but if at all possible it should be done. I am writing this chapter on a flight from Hong Kong, China, to Los Angeles. In the past week I had the privilege of preaching in several churches in Hong Kong. One of the highlights of the week was attending the missionary/national pastor prayer breakfast on Wednesday morning. Each week the independent Baptist missionaries and local pastors meet for prayer, breakfast, fellowship, and discussion. Not everyone is able to attend each week, but it is an opportunity to encourage each other and pray together as the Bible teaches. This particular week there were American, Chinese, Filipino, and Japanese pastors in attendance. These men were not meeting together to establish some type of hierarchy or pecking order. They are humble, Christ-like men of God who love each other and want to encourage each other in the work. Hong Kong is a city of seven million people in a small area with excellent transportation. I realize many fields would not be suitable to a weekly prayer breakfast like this.

Let me give you some practical advise for developing and maintaining good missionary relationships as you begin your ministry abroad.

1. Practice the Golden Rule as taught by the Lord Jesus Christ. Too often our version of the golden rule is "he with the most gold, rules." That is not the golden rule I am talking about! I am advocating the golden rule that Jesus taught, which is simply that we should treat others as we ourselves wish to be treated (Matthew 22:39). It is amazing what a difference it makes in our relationships with others when we treat them with the same respect that we wish to receive.

2. Rejoice when God chooses to bless another missionary or church. We need to understand that the work of God is bigger than our particular ministry. We need to learn to weep with those that weep and rejoice with those that rejoice. It takes the grace of God working in our lives to understand that it is okay for God to bless another brother, even if that means his church is larger than ours, or he has a nicer building than we do. A sovereign God knows what is best in these areas, and we need to learn to not be so competitive that we cannot honestly rejoice in another brother's blessings. The truth is that if we were more concerned with God's glory than our own, we would find it much easier to rejoice over someone else being blessed! God's blessings are plentiful enough to go around. There is enough for everyone.

3. Always be ethical in your personal dealings. Never try to persuade another worker to leave one ministry and help you with yours. In fact, not only should you not encourage it—you should not even allow it! If a national pastor contacts you as a missionary, desiring to leave another missionary's church to work with you, you should insist that it be done only with the other missionary's blessing. These are the type of unethical dealings that destroy relationships and hinder the work of Christ. People who love the Lord and want to please Him should live by a higher ethical standard.

Many years ago when I was a missionary in Hong Kong, I had the privilege of working with some extremely dedicated and talented Chinese pastors. One day a missionary that was not affiliated with us called my assistant pastor and offered him a church of his own if he would leave me and align himself with the other group. This was done without first speaking to me. This is the type of unethical dealings that drive a wedge between the very people who should be modeling ethical behavior to the national pastors and workers. Everyone loses when God's men do not act with integrity. In this particular case, my assistant did not accept the offer. This dear

Chinese brother was not a hireling looking for an opportunity to better himself. He was then, and is still today, a dedicated man of God, content to serve in whatever capacity the Lord wills.

Being ethical is more than simply a behavior to be exhibited among those engaged in ministry. It is a revelation of who you are at the innermost core of your being. God's servants are called to a higher standard of behavior. Leadership requires an understanding that we are never only our own persons. We belong to the one that we represent, and He will be judged by our behavior. That means if we are not ethical, if we cut corners and are not truthful, our Lord will be denigrated by those with whom we come in contact.

The missionary, and his counterpart in the ministry, the pastor, must remember that we never cease to be God's representatives. This is who we are. We are God-called ambassadors of Jesus Christ. This truth should drive us to our knees in humility and cause us to cry out with Paul, *"who is sufficient for these things?"* (2 Corinthians 2:16). The answer to that heartfelt cry is that none of us are sufficient in and of ourselves. We have this treasure in earthen vessels, and we must be filled with the Spirit and walk in daily surrender to Him if we are to represent Him well. We must never forget that we are being observed. Many years ago, I had an experience that God used to drive this truth home to my heart.

My family was living in a village in Hong Kong, China. We were studying Cantonese, which was the local dialect, and at the same time starting a local church by use of an interpreter. One day I felt that we needed a little "down time" as a family, so I decided to treat our family to an American hamburger. There was no place in our village to acquire such a delicacy, so we loaded everybody up for the journey into town and the tourist area where American fast food could be found. The trip was quite an ordeal. It began with a thirty-minute walk down the side of a mountain from our village to the train station. At the station, we fought the rush-hour crowds to purchase tickets and board a train for the standing-room-only ride into town, where we switched trains and stood like packed sardines for another thirty-minute ride into the tourist area. We finally arrived in the tourist area where the coveted fast food could be found. We jostled our way through the crowds (being careful not to lose one of our three young children) as we walked another twenty minutes through the ninety degree heat and humidity to the hamburger stand. The various train rides were punctuated by the body odor and stares of hundreds of people that all shared the same skin and hair pigmentation! My family attracted a lot of attention with our various hair and eye colors.

Finally we arrived at our destination, stood in line again, ordered our hamburgers, and found a table. The food was ready to eat, so we bowed our heads, thanked God for it, and began to eat. By this time I was not in a very good mood, so we sat mostly in silence eating our American hamburgers wondering if they were really worth all the effort and dreading the long trip back home.

About that time I noticed a lady at a neighboring table staring at us. I tried to ignore her, but by this time I had just about all the staring I could stand for one night! I turned and said to her in Cantonese, the local Chinese dialect, "Are you enjoying your food?"

Now the truth is I couldn't care less how her culinary experience was proceeding! I was sick and tired of being stared at, and my question was asked in sarcasm, not friendliness! Evidently she did not detect my bad spirit because she replied in Cantonese that she was enjoying her food. I thought the conversation was over, but to my utter shock she looked at me and said, "Are you a Christian?" I do not know if I have ever been so surprised by such a simple question. You would think that would not be a difficult question for a Baptist preacher to answer, but I was floored. I wanted to say "No, I am not a Christian. Christians do not act like me! They do not have bad attitudes like mine; Christians are Christ-like, and I am obviously not Christ-like." That is what I wanted to say, but that is not what I said. The Holy Spirit smote my heart with conviction about my bad attitude. I looked at her and said, "Yes, I am a Christian, are you?" She replied, "No I am not, but I thought you probably were because you can speak Cantonese. The business people and tourists normally do not learn to speak Chinese, only the missionaries."

God overruled my poor testimony and allowed me to witness to this dear lady. God was doing more than allowing me to witness to her; He was teaching me that I am never "off duty," when it comes to living the Christian life!

4. Do not engage in criticism of other ministries. I understand that there is a time and place for warning the flock to beware of false teachers and ministry philosophies. The Bible is clear that we must *"earnestly contend for the faith"* (Jude 3), and we are to expose error for the sake of protecting the flock (Acts 20:28–30). This should be done without fear or favor. God will hold His messengers responsible to faithfully deliver His message.

There is a major difference, however, between the defense of the truth and the petty criticism of another ministry. Petty criticism comes from petty spirits, while bold defense of the faith comes from a courageous heart. The former is motivated by insecurity and the latter by love. I am afraid that much of what we mask as a defense of the faith is in reality simply jealousy. Those of us in the ministry would be wise to ask God to help us to live by the spirit of Romans 14, where the Apostle Paul encourages us to refrain from setting ourselves up as judge and jury over God's servants. Consider these questions from the Holy Spirit.

Who art thou that judgest another man's servant? to his own master he standeth or falleth. Yea, he shall be holden up: for God is able to make him stand.—ROMANS 14:4

But why dost thou judge thy brother? or why dost thou set at nought thy brother? for we shall all stand before the judgment seat of Christ.—ROMANS 14:10

These are heart-searching questions. I am afraid that too many times in more than thirty years of ministry I have been guilty of setting myself up as the self appointed judge and jury of men and ministries that I had no business criticizing. I was talking about things of which I knew nothing and grieving the Spirit of God by my petty criticism of good men!

May God help us to know the difference between legitimate contending for the faith by rebuking error and illegitimate criticism of others! Think before you speak and ask yourself: Is it true? Is it necessary to repeat? Is it Christ-honoring for me to spread this bad report of another brother? If you can honestly say yes to those three questions, then have at it! If you cannot answer in the affirmative, it is probably best not to repeat it.

In this chapter we have discussed your relationship with other missionaries. May I encourage you to take the high road in this area and to honor the Lord in your spirit towards others. Be an encourager. Maintain a spirit of cooperation and brotherly encouragement when possible and a spirit of humble kindness when it is not. Above all, God will bless your ministry as a product of your right heart towards Him and towards others.

CHAPTER TEN

Learning the Language

Dwight Tomlinson

F*or if the trumpet give an uncertain sound, who shall prepare himself to the battle? So likewise ye, except ye utter by the tongue words easy to be understood, how shall it be known what is spoken? for ye shall speak into the air.*—1 CORINTHIANS 14:8–9

The study of your new language on the field must be given top priority for one simple reason: We are called to preach the Gospel, and words are the tools with which we communicate! It all boils down to being able to say the words. You must be able to communicate in a language that the people understand so they can know the wonderful love of God, manifested through the death, burial, and resurrection of His only begotten Son. That is the foundation of everything the missionary does. Remember that God sent His Son to earth, speaking the language of the people to whom He was sent. He did not expect them to learn a new language to discover the truth. God gave the truth to people in a language they could understand.

If we are to communicate the Gospel in a language they understand, that will mean **a** language other than English for much of the world's population. (English may very well be the universal language of the last days, but that does not mean that everyone speaks or understands it.)

You may be feeling as if you could never learn another language, but that is simply not so. One reason we feel so inadequate in learning another language is that very few native-born Americans are bilingual—in contrast to Europeans, most of whom speak two or three languages. Here in America the situation is different. Most ethnic groups learn to speak English after they are here for a generation, and the future generations often forget their mother tongue.

Many people who are no more intelligent or talented than you learn to communicate effectively in a language that is not their mother tongue. These people do not have some secret that is not available to you. They are not "lucky" or "wired so that it comes easily for them." Certainly there are some that will be able to learn a language a little easier than others. We are all created differently when it comes to natural ability and intelligence, but that does not mean that some can learn a second language and others cannot. If you have average intelligence and will apply yourself to the diligent study of the language, you will eventually learn to communicate.

It is also true that not all languages are equally difficult to learn. The easiest languages to learn are those which use the English alphabet as the base—such as French, German, Italian, Spanish, and other European languages. In many cases the pronunciation is similar if not identical. The farther removed from English, the more difficult the language becomes for the American missionary to learn.

For example, the tonal languages of Asia can be very intimidating at first. The untrained ear may not be able to discern anything that distinguishes one word from another. It sounds as if the native speaker is speaking very rapidly and the words make no sense at all. There must be thousands of unintelligible sounds and nuances that are impossible to learn. Take Chinese as an example. In Mandarin there are four tones; in Cantonese there are nine! The same word spoken in nine different tones will have nine different meanings. Obviously Chinese cannot be learned in "thirteen easy lessons."

Let me give you a few practical suggestions on this topic.

1. Make it a priority. Remember you must learn to communicate in a language they understand, and until you do, your ministry will be greatly limited.

2. Look at the big picture. Take time to be thorough. It is tempting to get just enough of the language to communicate on a superficial level and then quit studying. This is a mistake that you would one day deeply regret.

3. Use it or lose it. You must do your best to be immersed in the language and culture if you ever hope to be fluent. This can be especially difficult if the local workers are well versed in English. Remember, you are not there to help your national worker improve his English. He is there to help you improve your skills in his language. Insist that he speak to you in the language that you are attempting to learn. This will be frustrating at times and cannot be followed without exception, but it should be the rule and not the exception.

4. Study English now as a foundation for future language study. The better you understand the rules of your own language, the easier it is to understand the new language. In language school the instructors will often refer to a particular part of speech to help you understand the concept that he or she is teaching you in the new language. For example, if they say to you that a word acts as an adjective or as an adverb it will help if you understand the difference. The stronger your foundation in English, the easier it will be for you to learn the new language.

5. Keep a small notebook handy and jot down new words as you learn them. Over twenty years ago I was preaching through an interpreter in Hong Kong, China. At the time, I was studying Cantonese and understood most of what the interpreter was saying. In the midst of the message, I departed from my notes and paraphrased a statement made by John the Baptist. I said something to the effect of John saying that he was not worthy to unloose the shoes of the Son of God. When the interpreter translated, he said a word that I had never heard before. Immediately I wondered if it was the Cantonese word for *worthy*, because I understood everything else in the sentence. I paused and repeated the statement; again he used the same unfamiliar word. I made a mental note of it, and as soon as the service was over I jotted that word down in my notebook. Later when I asked the interpreter about it, I discovered that it was indeed the word *worthy*. To this day I remember the proper pronunciation for the word *worthy* in Cantonese. Write it down!

6. Write a brief testimony, invitation to church, and verse, and then memorize it in your new language. There is no reason that you can't at least introduce yourself and invite someone to church within the first couple of months. Many missionaries decide to wait until they really have a handle on the language before they start to invite people to church or try to communicate with people. Start with the basics and you will be amazed at how quickly your ability will grow.

7. Seek to learn five new words each service. Rather than letting your mind wander because you do not understand the preaching, consider obtaining a copy of the outline before the service and focus on learning the meaning of some of the words in that outline. Knowing a few of the words in the outline before the service starts will help you pick up new words just by virtue of the context during the service.

8. Take every opportunity possible to listen to translated preaching. This is especially helpful in learning the order of words and the structure of sentences in your new language.

9. Make it a lifelong habit. You will not attend language school all of your life, but you should choose to become a lifelong student of your adopted language.

10. Do not succumb to discouragement. Learning a new language is far from easy. You will be tempted many times to give up in despair. Remember that the frustration you feel is temporary. You *will* learn this language in time. Pray and trust God to bless your efforts. You are not the first person to feel like a total failure. Keep praying, and do not give up. Get out in the streets and use it. At first you will not be understood, but most people will appreciate that you are trying to speak their language! In time, you will find that something "clicks" and you begin to understand. Once that happens, you are well on your way to speaking and can look forward to eventually leading someone to Christ in his or her native tongue! When that first convert bows his head, confesses that he is a sinner, and calls upon the Lord Jesus Christ to save his soul, you will be so glad that you did not give up on learning the language.

J. Herbert Kane in his book *Life and Work on the Mission Field* mentions six obstacles to learning a new language:

1. Lack of self discipline
2. Lack of adequate opportunities for study
3. Lack of basic tools
4. Lack of qualified teachers
5. Too many interruptions
6. A tendency to discouragement

Learning a new language is no easy task, but it is a part of your calling. Although your efforts may take years and the process will sometimes seem overwhelming, commit yourself to the task and trust the Lord to strengthen you day by day. If you view your calling to the field as a life call, then taking a few years to master the language is relatively small in light of the many years you will serve the Lord on this field. The burden of learning the language will be far outweighed by the blessings of leading others to Christ in that language!

CHAPTER ELEVEN

Culture Shock

Paul Chappell

The term "culture shock" provokes a variety of responses. For example, many American pastors are feeling culture shock nearly every day as they observe the rapidly changing culture of America! To see a growing percentage of our citizenship in America piercing their noses, eyebrows, tongues, and cheeks can truly be shocking! Many of these same people are branding and tattooing their bodies and living lifestyles that would have only been seen in pagan cultures a few decades ago. While these sights are "shocking," they do not yet make up mainstream America.

Imagine, however, moving your wife and children to a country where branding, piercing, and other satanic activities are commonplace. Or, imagine moving them to a place where they are the only ones in an entire city with blond hair and blue eyes!

Culture shock evidences itself in many ways, depending upon the country to which God has called you.

The Reality of Culture Shock

The reality of culture shock must not be overlooked when considering God's call to a particular field. Every new missionary will face culture shock. It does not matter how many times you have visited the country as a tourist or on a short-term mission's trip. After a few months of residence in any foreign country, culture shock settles in as a reality for every missionary family.

As a fifteen-year-old boy, I can still recall taking our first family drive with my missionary parents around the city of Seoul, Korea. Seoul was beginning to modernize in the 1970s, but still had a long way to go. The sights and smells on that first family trip only hardened my already somewhat rebellious teenage heart. Thankfully, the Lord got a hold of my heart during our first year in Korea, and I enjoyed most of my time as a missionary kid.

The devil used these cultural differences in my teenage heart and tried to make me resent them and resent the Lord's leading in my family. Oftentimes, culture shock causes young people to respond with rebellion and resentment, while at the same time causing a wife to experience depression or discouragement. The wife's culture shock will present itself in myriad ways related to frustrations with shopping and caring for her family in a foreign country.

Some ways culture shock evidences itself are as follows:

Language

Culture shock first presents itself through "language shock." Establishing residence in a foreign land where you cannot communicate effectively is very difficult and discouraging at first. The inability to communicate can be overwhelming!

Sanitation

Many mission fields do not have water purification or sewage treatment plants. Hence, there is a need to boil water or drink bottled water and, in some cases, endure terrible odors!

Animosity toward the West

There is a growing animosity throughout the world toward America, and this is especially heightened in Muslim countries. While many countries are friendly toward Americans, it can be a shock for a patriotic American to realize how people in much of the world feel about America.

Shopping

Most foreign countries are not as developed in their grocery markets and shopping amenities as America. A missionary wife may have to learn how to shop in the open markets of Asia or in the very costly environments of Europe in order to provide for her family. Whether the high prices of a European country or difficulty finding good dairy products in Africa, these challenges will require great flexibility and endurance. Think of it this way—a missionary wife, in some sense, will have to develop a completely new system and adapt to a new culture in maintaining a household in a foreign land.

Immorality

While America is rapidly degenerating morally, many countries have far surpassed us in this terrible trend. It is not uncommon in European and Asian cities for prostitution to abound and for pornography to be even more readily available than it is in America. You must be spiritually prepared to fight this battle for your own heart and for your family. God will enable you and strengthen you, but you must anticipate the battle being stronger on a foreign field.

Spiritual Darkness

People who have lived for centuries in a godless and pagan society have a spiritual darkness upon their culture that is wicked and often barbaric. Depending on the country where you will be serving, this spiritual darkness could lead to many disturbing and alarming experiences for you and your family.

These are just a few categories in which one might expect culture shock. There are thousands of nuances particular to a given country—from driving in traffic to emergency and medical services to strange new foods and customs. I will never forget the first time I sat at a meal with a group of Asian pastors. One of them belched rather loudly. When I expressed some shock over this action, I was told it was a way to compliment the cook on having made a tremendous meal!

Other customs may include taking off one's shoes before entering a house, bowing upon meeting a new friend, or spitting into a tissue instead of spitting on the street. Every land has its own customs and culture, and every new missionary family will endure a season of "shock." Learning a new culture and adapting your lifestyle to new customs will require patience and steadfastness from the Lord.

The Remedy for Culture Shock

In 1 Corinthians 9:22, the Apostle Paul said, "*To the weak became I as weak, that I might gain the weak: I am made all things to all men, that I might by all means save some.*"

Without ever compromising his love for Christ or His doctrine, the Apostle Paul did everything he could to reach souls wherever he went. If we will reach souls on foreign soil, we too must be willing to adapt and humble ourselves in the will of God.

It is not your responsibility to transport American culture to foreign soil. When there are certain aspects of our culture that are biblically based, such as modesty, of course these should be taught to those who trust Christ as their Saviour. Modesty is a biblical principle. Wearing a tie, however, in the Philippines may or may not be considered a biblical principle. Many fine men of God in the Philippines preach in a dress shirt that is native to the Filipino culture. This type of shirt gives a sharp appearance and is not considered inappropriate by many great men of God.

It would be silly for a missionary to feel that he had to fight that part of the Filipino culture. Unfortunately, many fundamental, Bible-believing Baptists choose such issues as their point of division when they could be encouraging one another in the greater work of soulwinning. As you respond to culture shock, it is vital that you do not attempt to conform your converts to American culture. You must teach biblical principles and discern the difference between cultural preferences and biblical values. Where there is merely a cultural preference that does not displease the Lord, I would encourage you to adapt to that preference as the Apostle Paul did.

Dr. Don Sisk, director emeritus of Baptist International Missions, Inc. shares his comments, "In Japan I would allow the Japanese Christians to determine how we would do certain things. My rule was: if the Japanese way does not violate a biblical principle, we will do things that way; however, if it violates a biblical teaching, we will do it the biblical way. Therefore, when the transition took place in leadership from missionary to national pastor, it was a smooth transition. As missionaries, we should strive to become adopted members of the society we serve. We simply become members of the local church."

So, how can we remedy some of the challenges that you will face regarding culture shock?

First, develop a friendship with a senior missionary family whenever possible. This may require humbling one's self to learn from someone who is not from the same home church or Bible college; however, even as a student needs mentoring in Bible college, a young missionary couple will need some mentoring in the early days of the mission field.

A more experienced missionary wife will take a younger wife and show her where to shop and how much to expect to spend on various foods. The older missionary can take the younger missionary and help him by explaining the best methods for evangelism, where a car can be repaired, or how to obtain a permit to meet in a particular apartment complex for a Bible study.

A more experienced missionary can help a newer missionary keep things in perspective. When the Apostle Paul was stranded on the island of Malta, he experienced tremendous rejection by the native people who thought he was a murderer because a snake had bitten him on the hand. Ultimately, because Paul did not react in anger but was filled with the Spirit, the natives allowed him to preach the Gospel to them and many were healed and saved. God blessed Paul's Spirit-filled patience with a different culture.

As in America, we cannot expect the unregenerate person in a foreign land to understand the doctrines of Christ, much less what we may feel is a superior way of doing business or preparing meals. One must be willing to learn and be patient. A senior missionary couple can help in the learning and patience processes.

Second, keep a teachable spirit toward established Christian leaders in the country where you are ministering. A new missionary is always wise to find a fundamental pastor who was, perhaps, led to Christ by an American missionary thirty or forty years ago. Ask that pastor to help you and "show you the ropes" in how to do ministry. Spend as much time as you can with these men of God. Invite them and their families to your home. Go soulwinning with them or participate in evangelistic meetings with them. The remedy for culture shock will only come as you have a servant's heart and a teachable spirit.

Third, enjoy the new culture you will experience. Since my days as a teenager living in Korea, I have always had a fond place in my heart for the Korean people. I love Korean food, and I love the Korean culture.

It was a great joy for me to travel all across the Korean countryside. I traveled by train, plane, and even a ten-speed bicycle, learning more about the recorded history of more than four thousand years.

There are games, foods, and customs that are unique to every country. If you believe God has called you to a country, you should take interest in those games, foods, and customs in order to be able to witness to the people more effectively.

Wherever you are around the world, if you express a love for the language, food, or customs of any people, you will always have a more ready audience when it comes time to preach the Gospel of Jesus Christ.

Fourth, establish your home as an American home. While I totally agree that a missionary family should embrace and learn from the culture around them, there is nothing wrong with having a little bit of America inside the four walls of your residence.

Many mothers will pack their missionary crates with items that will remind them and their children of their homeland. Young boys may want to decorate their rooms with the colors of a favorite sports team. Young girls may want to decorate their rooms with some other reminders of home. As often as possible, it is good to have an American meal, remember American holidays, and have devotions in English with your family on a regular basis.

Many missionaries around the world watch the services at Lancaster Baptist Church via live streaming video. This has allowed their families to hear preaching in English and to feel a connection with a church in their homeland. In recent years, I have seen many missionaries coming back to the States almost too frequently, in my opinion. Trips back home can be helpful and often necessary, yet it is wise for a missionary family to take only those trips they deem essential. These trips could ultimately serve to prolong culture shock and to keep your entire family from truly embracing the call of God to a foreign land.

For example, there may be a significant event in the life of a family member, such as a fiftieth wedding anniversary, the death of a relative, or the graduation of your child from high school. These significant moments should be remembered and attended if possible. In today's global economy with air transportation quite affordable, it is not wrong to take opportunity to spend time in America for those special medical and personal moments.

The key is balance. A missionary can overemphasize maintaining American culture or visiting America to the point that it prevents his family from settling in, establishing a fruitful ministry, and truly making a difference on the foreign field.

The Reversal of Culture Shock

Perhaps you have heard the phrase "reverse culture shock." Reverse culture shock is a real dilemma which will be faced by every family who has spent even a few years on the mission field.

I remember returning home from Korea as a teenage boy and thinking, "Wow, American people are really fat. Everywhere I look people look obese!" There is very little obesity in Korea, and while the obesity in America probably had not changed significantly while I was away, it was one of the first things I noticed.

A high school friend of mine had grown up in Korea all of his life. He had made relatively few trips to America during his upbringing. Upon completion of high school his parents sent him back to the States for college. It was about three months into his college experience that we received word from his family that he had committed suicide.

My friend literally felt like a stranger in his own country. For example, he did not understand American sarcasm. Many times people would make jokes that he did not think were funny. He felt awkward in his verbal communication and felt like a complete failure when it came to dating and social circumstances.

In addition, my friend did not have a good support system around him. The tragic loss of his life is something from which every missionary can learn.

With the inventions of VCRs, DVDs and now live-streaming video, most American families can keep in touch with good aspects of our culture while they are overseas. We often send preaching videos, youth conference videos, and DVDs to missionaries who are raising teenagers. This allows the teenagers to hear, firsthand, some of the ways the devil is fighting teenagers in America and, subsequently, they are more prepared when they arrive home.

Not long ago, a missionary family brought their child to West Coast Baptist College from the country of Japan. I noticed that they checked into a hotel and stayed in our area for nearly three weeks. They took their daughter to Wal-Mart, the mall, and several restaurants. They visited with our church families and spent time getting to know all of the teachers. This family had a special meeting with me to introduce me to their daughter, and we hosted them in our home for a meal.

The parents told me they wanted to be familiar with the area where their daughter would spend the next four years during college. They helped us know some of the needs their daughter would have, and we have done our best to meet those needs along the way. They made sure their daughter had some friends before they left, and of course, they have kept in constant touch with her since returning to Japan.

Several years ago, a missionary friend of mine met with me when he brought his daughter to our college from Papua New Guinea. He said, "Brother Chappell, please keep an eye on our daughter as she transitions back into the American culture." He told me, "She knows more about how to handle snakes and chop wood with a machete than how to date boys!"

His daughter made a wonderful transition, due to his very thorough help, counsel, and support through the process. Today, she is married to a fine young preacher and together they are being greatly used of God in full-time ministry.

Do not diminish in your mind the seriousness of reverse culture shock. When it comes time to return to the States, be sure you do not merely rush from church to church and place to place. Be sure that you have scheduled time for your family to assimilate back into their own home culture.

As we close this chapter, I want to thank God for the power of the Gospel in every culture. The Gospel message was one that changed the lives of Jews, Gentiles, and Samaritans in the first century. The Gospel is changing lives around the world today.

While many in today's religious circles are trying to adapt their messages to the culture, may we realize the purpose of the church is not to adapt Christ to men, but to adapt men to Christ. No matter which culture we live in, the goal is always Christ-likeness.

Culture shock is a very real and difficult part of missions. Many have gone before you and have exhibited that God will give sustaining grace through the culture shock! You will survive and your family will thrive in God's call if you will trust Him and patiently wait upon His renewing strength. Through both "culture shock" and "reverse culture shock," may God grant you wisdom and power as you lead others to conform to the image of Christ!

PART FOUR

Doing the Work of
a Missionary

CHAPTER TWELVE

Church Planting

Dwight Tomlinson

Biblical missions is church planting. The two cannot be separated. The Great Commission is clear that the first church was to reproduce itself by winning souls, baptizing the converts, and then teaching those baptized believers to perpetuate the work of Christ by reproducing other churches (Matthew 28:16–20). The local New Testament church has been given the responsibility to start other local churches, and that is precisely the reason local Baptist churches send out missionaries. We send them out for the express purpose of winning souls and building indigenous local churches. What is an "indigenous church"? In order to truly be considered indigenous, the church must be three things.

Self-supporting
Self-propagating
Self-governing

Any local church that does not have these three characteristics cannot be truly considered to be an indigenous work. In a very real sense, the job of a missionary is to work himself out of a job. This is the difference between the calling of a pastor and the calling of a missionary. Ephesians chapter four mentions several ministerial callings. Two of them are still active today. It is my belief that the two callings in Ephesians that are still active today are pastor/teacher and evangelist. It is my opinion that the reference to an evangelist is the position that we normally refer to as a missionary.

The pastor has a calling to stay at one church teaching the Word of God to the congregation. Pastors are also told to "do the work of an evangelist" so we must never lose our heart for soulwinning and church planting; however, the primary difference between the missionary and the pastor is the fact that the missionary does not stay at one church his entire life. He starts a church and works to bring it to an indigenous position. Then he goes to a different area and does it again. The best Bible example of this work in action is the great missionary, Paul.

If this is not the case, then we must ask the question: What is the difference between a pastor and a missionary? Why do we use different terms for the two offices? Why am I called a pastor and a missionary called a missionary? Is it just because one serves in America and the other does not? Why would the Bible give one title for a man who serves locally while calling the same man by a different title if he serves away from home?

I have had the privilege of starting three independent Baptist churches during my thirty-plus years of ministry. Two of them are in America and one of them is in Hong Kong, China. Why was I considered a pastor for two of them and a missionary for one, unless the difference was in purpose? When I started the Redwood Baptist Church in Redwood City, California, and the Bay Area Baptist Church in Newark, California, it was my intention to stay at those churches as the pastor. God had other plans, but my intention was to stay. When I started the Bible Baptist Church in Hong Kong my intention was to someday turn the church over to a national pastor. That is, in essence, the biblical difference between a pastor and a missionary, in my opinion. I realize that some will take a different position on these titles, which is why I stress that this is my *opinion*. If you see it differently, that is fine with me, and good men can differ on these things. My suggestion would be "*...let every man be fully persuaded in his own mind*" (Romans 14:5), and I am persuaded that a missionary should seek to work himself out of a job by leading a church to be indigenous! With that introduction, let us jump into the practical steps of local church planting on the mission field.

Look Before You Leap

Most new missionaries work with a veteran missionary for a period of time before starting a new church. There are many beneficial reasons for this. Mentoring under another provides time to learn the language and customs of the people. It gives you an opportunity to experience some culture shock while you are not as likely to do and say things that you will regret later. It gives you time to pray and seek the area to which God will direct you. These and many other reasons would indicate that it is wise to work with another missionary for some period of time before starting a new church. This will not always be possible, but if so, it is normally the best course of action.

The amount of time spent working with another missionary will vary depending upon the difficulty of language study, the readiness of the new missionary, and the working of the Holy Spirit. Some missionaries arrive on the field expecting to study the language and help another missionary only to find out that the Holy Spirit has already arranged everything for the new church to be planted almost immediately. I preached in one thriving church in Asia where the missionary started his church much earlier than he had planned.

This particular missionary had not even completely unpacked his boxes when he heard a knock on his front door. At the door was a young man who asked the American if he was a missionary, and if so, would he be willing to teach the Bible to him and his family! Needless to say, the church started much sooner than the missionary planned. This is an unusual case, but we must never forget that our plans are always susceptible to change by God.

You must realize that God is already at work in the hearts and lives of people before you arrive on the field. The Holy Spirit is preparing the soil for your efforts, and your call is but a small piece of the bigger picture of what God is already doing on your field. All of our best laid plans and strategies must often be set aside when God's hand so obviously intervenes. You must be sensitive to the Lord's working above all and follow the leading of the Holy Spirit in these matters.

When You Do Start, Do It Right

All Christian service should be done with the highest possible ethical behavior. If a new missionary has been working with an older missionary for a period of time before starting his own work, the new missionary has an obligation to receive the counsel and advice of the older missionary before starting. It would be unethical to secretly solicit several people from the church, move down the street and use them to start a new church. Notice I used the word, "secretly." If the other pastor is willing and able to sponsor such an endeavor, that is wonderful, but it should be done under the direction of the Holy Spirit, not by coercion.

> *But have renounced the hidden things of dishonesty,*
> *not walking in craftiness, nor handling the word of*
> *God deceitfully; but by manifestation of the truth*
> *commending ourselves to every man's conscience in*
> *the sight of God.*—2 Corinthians 4:2

If the Lord leads the existing church to send some of its members to help plant a new church, everyone wins. Churches should plant other churches, and the Lord will bless the church and pastor that are willing to reproduce in this manner. The important thing for the new missionary to keep in mind is that he must not usurp the authority of the pastor or split a church in order to start a new work. God will not bless a ministry that is founded in direct contradiction to His Word.

If the missionary or national pastor you have been working with is not willing to help you start a new work, move to another needy city and start it by yourself. The Lord will use you to establish the work. He called you and He knows already who He is going to bring into your life to help you get started. We can never go wrong looking to and trusting the Lord of the harvest.

Getting Started

Once you have discerned that God is leading you to step out and start the new work, there are several things you should do in the planning stages.

1. Pray and Ask God to Direct You to a City or Area Where You Should Plant the New Church

While it is true that you cannot take the Gospel to the wrong address, it is also true that God has a specific place where He desires to place you. Church planting is too important to be done in an unspiritual manner. Spend some time fasting, praying, and seeking God's direction on where you should start the new church. Abraham's servant was able to say, *"I being in the way, the Lord led me"* (Genesis 24:27). Every church planter needs that same confidence as he faces the inevitable discouragements that come in church planting.

2. Find a Place for You and Your Family to Live and Begin Making Contacts in the Community

This can be done through the normal process of getting settled somewhere. The person who helps you at the bank, the people from which you rent your home, people you meet in the market place—these are all good prospects for the Gospel and to attend your new church. When my wife and I were getting started in Hong Kong, we would deliberately go to lunch at the most crowded time of the day. The custom in busy Hong Kong restaurants is to seat people at the same table even if they are not together. They simply roll up one corner of the tablecloth, put a new tablecloth on that section of the table, and seat different parties at the same table! That makes for an efficient, if somewhat uncomfortable seating arrangement according to western standards. For my wife and me, it was perfect! We had a captive audience sitting across the table from us!

3. Determine How to Handle the Language Barrier

Will you preach with an interpreter or use the native language yourself? If you are going to use an interpreter, it will be important to develop that person's communication skills. They should be able to effectively communicate the message with enthusiasm and compassion, and they should have a good working relationship with you. Your translator is very important. Do your best to have a good understanding and appreciation of one another.

4. Find and Secure a Meeting Place

This will probably be a rented building at first. When our family started the Bible Baptist Church of Hong Kong, we began in our home. After several months of meeting in our home we rented the third and fifth floors of a commercial building in a section of Hong Kong called "Mong Gok" (crowded corner). We would have rented two floors together, but the Hong Kong Bartenders Association already had the fourth floor! Eventually we purchased an apartment in the same area and converted it into a meeting place.

Wherever you start, make the meeting place as attractive and conducive to ministry as possible. Think through the arrangements that will be needed such as nurseries, childcare, auditorium, etc., and make sure you choose a building that will be adequate.

5. Make Sure Your Children's Education Is in Place

Do not sacrifice your family while getting the new church started. There are many excellent home school and educational programs that missionaries can use successfully on the field should they be needed. Be sure that your children have what they need to grow and prepare for their future.

6. Print Tracts with Your Address and Contact Information Readily Available

This would include the location and times of services and a way to contact someone for additional information.

7. Decide on Order and Frequency of Services

Will you meet on Sunday morning only at first? Or will you meet both Sunday morning and evening? Will there be a midweek service, Sunday school program, nursery, etc.?

8. Arrange Music

Music is a vital part of worship, and you should do your best to have a quality music program of *"singing and making melody on your hearts to the Lord"* (Ephesians 5:19) right from the beginning. The music program may be as basic as you and your family singing hymns from the hymnal. Do not underestimate the simplicity and power of such worship! Remember, the music program is about obeying and worshipping the Lord in sincerity, not about entertaining visitors or impressing attendees.

9. Secure Literature, Bibles, Hymnals and Other Things You Will Need to Aid in the Services

10. Print and Distribute Thousands of Flyers for the Opening Service

This is probably best done within two or three weeks from the opening service. Too far before that will allow too much time, and people will forget that a new church is starting. Get out into the area as much as possible prior to starting. Meet anyone and everyone. Invite every person you meet to visit your new church. Be aggressive about spreading the word!

11. Prepare the Direction of the Messages in Advance

In other words, do not just wing it. Be prepared. The Holy Spirit can as easily lead you in advance as He can on a Saturday night in the preparation of messages. If you have a short series of four to six weeks, you might be able to get some folks back that would have only attended once. Think well ahead in your sermon series development and preparation. The more powerful your messages, the more fruit you will see in the work.

12. Prepare a Detailed Checklist and Work Your Way through It to Make Sure You Are Prepared for the Opening Service

Do not leave anything to memory. Write it down and go over your checklist.

13. Be Winning Souls before the Church Gets Started

God will most likely give you new converts if you are seeking to win them prior to the starting of your church. I am amazed as I think of many missionary friends who have shared stories of the first souls they led to Christ on the mission field. Often, these new Christians become key leaders in the work that God is growing. Keep your heart soft and keep the Gospel on the tip of your tongue!

14. Disciple the People You Are Leading to Christ

As you lead people to Christ, do not wait until the church begins to start following up and discipling those new Christians. Whether it is in your home or in some other setting, make deliberate attempts to immediately begin nurturing and developing the people that you have led to Christ.

15. Pray Much for God's Power and Blessing

What can possibly replace God's anointing and favor upon your efforts? Above all, we must have God's power in this work! Prayer is that which turns your human strategies and labor into the divinely blessed work and touch of God. Commit yourself to faithful and consistent prayer for God's blessing and favor upon your labor.

16. If Possible, Begin the Church with a National Pastor at Your Side

This is not always possible, but it is always preferable to begin a work with a national pastor working with you. When we started the church in Hong Kong, we were not able to do this. We did not yet know a Chinese man who was called and ready to plant a new church. In fact, we did not have any help at all.

We began in our home and had one Chinese man attend the first service. As time went by, God brought into our lives the young man that He wanted to take my place. This all happened more than twenty years ago, and that Chinese pastor and I are still very close friends. He has proven to be a solid, dependable man of God.

Indigenous, a Goal or a Method?
Contributed by Dr. Don Sisk

Missionaries have always wrestled with the problem of how much money the missionary should use in establishing a church on the mission field. Most independent Baptist missionaries have a goal of establishing an indigenous church; however, there is much confusion even among fundamental Baptists over the word *indigenous*. The word *indigenous* means "produced, growing, or living naturally in a country or climate; thus native." The word is often used concerning plants or trees. We say that certain plants or trees grow naturally in this country, or that this plant or tree is native or indigenous to this country. For instance, cherry blossom trees are indigenous to Japan. In the Antelope Valley, we would say that Joshua trees and tumbleweeds are indigenous.

I suppose in the strictest sense of the word there is no such thing as an indigenous church. The church does not grow naturally anywhere. The church is a supernatural work of God. In Matthew 16:18 Jesus said, *"...upon this rock I will build my church; and the gates of hell shall not prevail against it."*

In theological terminology when we speak of an indigenous church, we are speaking of a church which has become financially self-supporting, self-governing, and self-propagating. This means the church would not receive financial help from outside sources, would not be influenced or dictated to by any higher ecclesiastical authority, and would be self-propagating, meaning they would reproduce themselves. As independent Baptists we believe that every church should be autonomous and that there is no ecclesiastical authority higher than the local church.

Concerning finances, there are some who would say that from the very beginning a church should be indigenous, meaning that the missionary should not put any funds into establishing the new church. If this was the case, there would be no such thing as a foreign missionary. When a missionary goes into a city, preaches the Gospel, baptizes those who are being saved, and teaches them, this is not natural or native to that particular area. Thus, to say from the very beginning the church must be indigenous would mean that there could be no foreign influence or in the strictest sense, no foreign missionaries. No church started by a foreign missionary is self-supporting, self-governing, or self-propagating from the very beginning. If the foreign missionary cannot put any financial support into the church, he also should not influence the governing of the church or the propagation of the church.

From the beginning of a new church, the missionary must be careful that he does not make the new church totally dependent upon his influence and his finances. He should have as a goal that one day this church would become an indigenous church, but he must realize that it will take some investment to get it there.

After thinking much and hearing many discussions on this subject, I believe the concept of being indigenous is a great goal; however, it is not a method. Let me explain with a simple illustration. God has given my wife and me two children. From the very beginning, we visualized that one day our children would be self-supporting (they would be able to provide for themselves), self-governing (they would be capable of making decisions for themselves), and self-propagating (they would reproduce themselves). However, we did not insist from the time of their births that they would be self-supporting, self-governing, and self-propagating. I knew that for some years I would be responsible for supporting and governing them, and for many years they would certainly not be self-propagating. But I had a goal that one day they would be.

God allowed us to start two churches in Japan. From the very beginning, my goal was that these churches would one day be totally indigenous. However, this did not mean that from the beginning I could not put my tithes and offerings into that local congregation, and it certainly did not mean that I could not influence the governing of that small, young church. I also did not expect them to reproduce another church in a matter of a few days. However, I believed that eventually these churches would become self-supporting, self-governing, and self-propagating.

God has wonderfully worked in both of these churches, and both of them today are indigenous. They do not receive any funds from outside sources, nor are they ruled by any other authority. One of the churches has started seven other churches in Japan and has thirteen missionary families on foreign mission fields. The other church has started three other churches in Japan and has three missionary families on foreign mission fields. Thus, the goal is being reached.

I feel that to have said from the beginning that I would not help support this church in any way whatsoever would not have been right. I do not believe that I violated a biblical principle by helping to financially support these churches at the beginning, nor do I believe that I violated a biblical principle by influencing the way the churches were governed.

At the start of those ministries, I was responsible for all the finances. I paid for the advertisements that went into the first meetings. I purchased handbooks and Bibles with money that had been raised for missions, and when it became necessary, I purchased chairs and other things that were needed for the start of the new church. In the beginning I made all the decisions. I chose and purchased the land on which the first church built their first building. Today this church is in their third location. In the last two locations, with money raised from their members, they have bought land and paid for their own buildings. In the other church, their building was a part of the property of our Bible school; however, after several years, the church desired to pay for the building they were using. The money was placed into a fund that helped start other new churches.

Many who talk about indigenous churches never establish indigenous churches. The most important thing is for the missionary to pray and seek God's guidance in any particular location as to how much or how little foreign money should go into the new church. Again, we must be very careful that we do not make the church dependent on American influence and money.

Dr. T. Stanley Soltau states in his book *Missions at the Crossroads*, "A church is not indigenous until it becomes native to the country and grows there naturally as a part and partial of the people among whom it has been planted." I feel that, in the case of the two churches mentioned above, this goal has been and is being met.

The indigenous policy is certainly spelled out in the Great Commission: *"Go ye therefore, and teach all nations, baptizing them in the name of the Father, and of the Son, and of the Holy Ghost: Teaching them to observe all things whatsoever I have commanded you: and, lo, I am with you alway, even unto the end of the world"* (Matthew 28:19–20). The Lord has commissioned us to evangelize, to baptize those who are being saved, and to teach those who have been evangelized and baptized to go evangelize and baptize others. This is the indigenous policy. I have often said that evangelism is not complete until the *evangelized* become the *evangelists*.

The American missionary is doing a great injustice to the churches planted in foreign countries if he does not teach them the biblical principles of giving. Soon after a church is established, the missionary should begin to teach the new converts to tithe. Luke 6:38 was not written for affluent Americans: *"Give, and it shall be given unto you; good measure, pressed down, and shaken together, and running over, shall men give into your bosom."* This is a promise from God to everyone who will give regardless of his income, the economic condition of his country, or his geographical location. Failing to teach new converts to give would be doing them an injustice.

By the same token, to have a superior attitude and feel that only American missionaries are capable of making spiritual decisions would be a great mistake. We must treat the national pastors as equals in the ministry and realize that the God who has equipped us to lead will equip those whom He chooses to lead in the new ministries.

In recent years, it has been a great joy to see churches even in third world countries sending missionaries around the world. I believe that in the independent Baptist missionary movement, the indigenous policy is working. In a recent conference on the island of Mindanao, several hundred national pastors met, and the emphasis of the entire meeting was for the churches on the island of Mindanao to send missionaries around the world. It was very obvious from that conference, which incidentally was called "Mindanao Conference on World Evangelism," that the indigenous policy is indeed very effective. In the beginning of those churches, the missionaries had a great influence. They gave most of the finances to start the churches; however, the churches have now become self-supporting, self-governing, and are starting new churches in the Philippines, as well as sending missionaries around the world.

As in most areas, balance is very important. Dr. C.C. Ryrie in his book *Balancing the Christian Life* makes this statement, "The main thing is to keep the main thing the main thing." I believe this is also true in the matter of establishing new churches on the mission fields. The main thing is that one day these new churches will learn the biblical principles of tithing and giving of offerings and will be able to support their pastors and their building programs. It is also the goal that God will raise up leaders who will be able to lead their people to make the right decisions for the churches. In time, the church should see the necessity of starting new churches in their homeland as well as sending missionaries around the world.

To perpetually support national pastors and never teach those churches their responsibilities and the joy of supporting their national pastors is indeed a great misuse of missions money and a great injustice to the national churches. However, to insist that these new churches must be indigenous from the very beginning is foolish. May God grant us the wisdom to know how much or how little American finances should be put into national works.

When it comes to church planting on a foreign field, there is no "one size fits all." Every field is very different and unique to itself. The best textbook is the book of Acts. Here, we trace the journeys of the great Apostle Paul as he traversed Asia Minor planting churches. At one point, he began a church with a group of ladies he had won to Christ by a riverbank. Another time he began with a jailer and his family. At one location he met in a schoolhouse for almost two years. Each culture, each city, and each church was unique to itself.

The common denominator in each of the churches he planted was prayer, preaching, and personal soulwinning. One example is found in Acts 14:21–23 which records the activity of the first missionary team. Notice what they did. First, they evangelized the lost and made disciples through the preaching of the Word of God. Second, they edified the believers through confirming or strengthening them, and through exhorting and warning them. Third, they established churches. They prayerfully chose leaders and delegated the ministry to the national leadership of the church. They trusted that the Lord, whom they had believed, would lead and sustain the new church.

Just get out and get started—then hang on for dear life with a bulldog tenacity that refuses to accept defeat and let God do whatever He pleases!

CHAPTER THIRTEEN

Training National Workers

PAUL CHAPPELL

Second Timothy 2:2 says, *"And the things that thou hast heard of me among many witnesses, the same commit thou to faithful men, who shall be able to teach others also."*

It strikes me that the primary focus of the Lord Jesus Christ was to train twelve men, and the primary focus of the apostle Paul was to train others—especially Timothy. Every ministry should have a philosophy of leadership training in order to perpetuate the Gospel ministry. If we are not constantly perpetuating leadership and teaching the doctrine of the Word of God, then we are hindering the future of Gospel ministry.

Every man of God must come to a point in his life and ministry when he realizes that he is passing the baton of the Christian faith to the next generation. May this chapter help you to develop a ministry philosophy that involves training leaders through your missions efforts who will carry the faith to future generations.

The Pastor's Responsibility

Developing leaders is not merely a matter of the health and growth of the church. It is a matter of the health and growth of the pastor. If a pastor is not developing other leaders around him, then he is the sole person that everyone in the congregation comes to for counsel, for advice, and for crisis intervention. It is vital that we develop leaders around us. If you expect to see God grow the church to more than fifty to one hundred folks, you must have other people that can help nurture the congregation.

I know this goes against what is taught in some circles, but simply put, I am not the sole expert in every area of life and ministry at Lancaster Baptist Church. I believe God has called me to be the primary spiritual leader. It is my duty to be an expert in areas of doctrine, church administration, prayer, and counsel of the staff and the leadership of the church. However, we have several leaders on our team who provide counsel in areas of finance, marriage, family, and personal needs. While I stay closely involved with our church family, many years ago I realized the necessity of having qualified men and women who could counsel in these areas. We have a lady on our staff who is in her fifties and has become an expert in counseling the women of our church. The Bible declares that older women should counsel the younger women of the church. My wife also does much of this.

As a pastor, you must develop a philosophy of leadership that reproduces and develops leaders around you. God will greatly multiply your ministry as you do.

The Purpose of Developing Leaders

The purpose of developing leaders in the ministry is to glorify Christ. Beyond this, the purpose is to bring growth into the life of believers. No one is really growing in the Christian life until they are participating in the ministry. Someone once said, "Tell me and I will forget, show me and I will remember, involve me and I will understand." My heart is to develop people in the ministry who understand the biblical philosophy and purpose of ministry, including soulwinning, separation, and church structure. New Christians will never understand the ministry to this degree unless they get involved—unless we intentionally develop them.

We must have a desire to help others around us to reach their full potential. If God would allow us the privilege to help twenty-five or fifty or one hundred or more men and women to truly reach their potential in spiritual leadership, we would ultimately see many others gathering around these, and all of us together following the Lord Jesus Christ.

We see this admonition in Ephesians 4:11–12, *"And he gave some, apostles; and some, prophets; and some, evangelists; and some, pastors and teachers; For the perfecting of the saints, for the work of the ministry, for the edifying of the body of Christ."* This is a familiar verse to all of us, and although we often have a heart to equip the saints for the ministry, we can easily discover that we are not doing so in a number that is necessary to take the church on to the next level for the cause of Christ. If we will effectively pass the baton, we must become aggressive about developing leaders around us.

This passage teaches us that one of the responsibilities of a church leader is to "equip the saints"—to mature the saints—to bring them to the place that they are no longer receiving just the milk of the Word, but they are receiving the meat of the Word and then with that nourishment, they are being able to exercise their God-given gifts for the ministry. This is what God means when He says, *"for the perfecting of the saints, for the work of the ministry."*

One of the statements that we have adopted for our staff regarding the development of leaders in the local church is the saying, "It is only as we develop others around us that we permanently succeed." The word success is only found once in the Bible, and it is a direct result of meditating on and obeying the Word of God. I believe these two truths tie together as God's Word instructs us to *"commit thou to faithful men, who shall be able to teach others also."* For biblical success to be realized, we must be constantly developing others around us—constantly discipling new converts so that they can go forward into the twenty-first century with the Gospel.

If we are going to accomplish this goal, we must have a strategy for doing so. One of the tragedies of today is that men have a vision for what they would like to see accomplished, but they have no strategy to accomplish that vision. Thank God for dreams and visions and goals, but vision without strategy is nothing more than good intentions. Good intentions never changed the world! We must have a strategy for biblical leadership development in the local church. It is the strategy that will take theory and translate it into action and eventually reality! Strategy is the road map that allows men to implement God's vision and see it come to reality by His grace.

The Identification and Selection of Leaders

The first step is selecting leaders in the church. In Acts 6:3–5, the Bible says, *"Wherefore, brethren, look ye out among you seven men of honest report, full of the Holy Ghost and wisdom, whom we may appoint over this business. But we will give ourselves continually to prayer, and to the ministry of the word. And the saying pleased the whole multitude: and they chose Stephen, a man full of faith and of the Holy ghost, and Philip, and Prochorus, and Nicanor, and Timon, and Parmenas, and Nicolas a proselyte of Antioch."* Here we notice the selection of the first servant leaders of the church—the deacons of the church of Jerusalem. I believe one of the jobs of a pastor, especially during his early days, is to begin to look for and select future leaders for the team.

As I sit in church on Sunday mornings and Sunday nights, I usually take mental notes so I can send "I missed you" letters to those who were absent. At the same time, as I look out over the congregation, I am dreaming and praying that God would use these wonderful people in a great and mighty way. It is often during these times that God will lay a particular person on my heart who He would desire to use in some specific way in ministry.

Only once in thirteen years have we put an article in the bulletin that said, "we need nursery workers," or "we need Sunday school workers." Call the church this week." Though I believe in a strong volunteer spirit, I do not believe that is how the Holy Spirit selects leaders. I believe that God is concerned with the spiritual development and growth of a person before they are placed into leadership. We must carefully seek to understand where a person is spiritually and pray for wisdom in placing them into leadership. Many years ago, God led us to establish a specific philosophy and some guiding policies in the area of selecting and choosing those who will be involved in church leadership. Here are a few guidelines.

First, we practice the principle of proving. We see this principle of proving in Acts 6. These men were from the congregation and they had obviously proven themselves to be godly men. God admonishes us in 1 Timothy 5:22 to *"Lay hands suddenly on no man...."* God is teaching us to have a season—a process of proving—before putting someone into the ministry.

Second, we practice the principle of credibility. The Scripture speaks of men being "of honest report." These were men who had a good testimony. They had credibility and integrity.

Third, we must seek spirituality. These were men who were "full of the Holy Ghost." As you seek potential leaders, look for those men whose hearts and dispositions are obviously filled and controlled by the Holy Spirit of God.

For instance, one evidence of the Holy Spirit's filling would be a heart for souls. One of the requirements for our leaders at Lancaster Baptist Church is that they be involved in reaching souls on a weekly basis. A spiritual leader with a right heart would not argue this.

Fourth, look for wisdom. The Bible says, *"men full of the Holy Ghost and wisdom."* While there may be some positions of service where less discernment is needed, working with people and teaching the Word of God requires great wisdom.

A wise man or woman will make potentially big problems smaller and potentially small blessings big! I am not saying they will minimize or disregard the hurts or trials of others. I am saying they will seek to resolve problems and heal them, rather than enlarge them. A carnal Christian, on the other hand, will take a small problem and enlarge it. The slightest thing "ticks them off"— the slightest thing starts their rampage.

Fifth, look for a humble servant's heart. In this passage it says *"whom we may appoint over this business."* In other words, these were servant leaders who would carry out directives from the apostles. This required that these men have true humility and a desire to serve. Barnabas was an encourager, one who came alongside others and helped them to reach their full potential.

The best way to find these kinds of people in your church is to be this kind of person *yourself*. A servant's heart is better *caught* than *taught*. One of my first jobs as pastor of Lancaster Baptist Church was to clean the toilets every Saturday evening. I am not sure that I knew what I was doing, but I did know how to put cleaner in the sinks so the church would smell clean when people walked in on Sunday morning. It might not have always been clean, but it smelled clean! Do not allow any ministry responsibility to be "beneath you." Have an attitude of a humble spirit and a servant's heart. This spirit will always be contagious.

A godly leader finds strength by realizing his weaknesses, grows into authority by being under authority, develops vision by seeing the needs of others, gains credibility by being an example to others, earns loyalty by expressing compassion, discovers honor by being faithful, and descends into greatness by being a servant.

Sixth, and finally, look for an active faith. The Bible says that they chose Stephen, a man full of faith. I believe that ministry leaders must be *"full of faith"*—faith in action. These men were actively involved in seeing the Word and the work of God go forward. They were not interested in politics and prestige. They were simply living out a dynamic faith in Jesus Christ.

It is vital that we spend time with people. You can impress people from a distance, but we can only influence them up close. Identifying and selecting leaders takes time and requires that you create environments in your ministry life when you can spend time getting to know people.

Just as Jesus spent time with His disciples—mentoring, training, praying with, and encouraging them—even so we have endeavored to identify leaders by identifying with people through hospitality and fellowship. The pastors of our church host people into their homes nearly every Sunday evening for the purpose of fellowship and encouragement. This is a part of the fiber of our ministry philosophy. People need encouragement. New Christians need to see what a real Christian home is like. People need to be around us if they are going to see what the Christian life is all about.

Yet for this to happen, we must be willing to identify with people—to connect with them personally. At one point in my ministry, I had the impression that a pastor had to have some kind of mystique—for example I thought I should wear wing tips and a tie to Home Depot! Let me challenge you with something—avoid the mystique mistake. If there is going to be a mystique in your life, God will put it there. Do not try to develop it yourself. You will have to be careful with balance—I understand that. But you will not impact lives if you do not spend time with people. And time with people is what God will use to identify leadership qualities in someone's heart. There are a number of different ways that you can create environments to identify emerging or potential leaders in your ministry. Here are a few ideas to get you started. You may have to adapt these to your own ministry or field, but allow the Holy Spirit to lead you in creating times where you can identify personally with the people.

Conduct a quality time of men's leadership training. We have done this since the very first months of Lancaster Baptist Church. In fact, at our first meeting we had three men—one of them was our head usher who is still serving faithfully today. At least three times a year, the men of Lancaster Baptist Church gather for an evening of leadership training, great food, and "iron-sharpening-iron" fellowship. These times have become critical to developing the spirit and leadership of our church family.

Conduct a quality ladies' fellowship. For many years, my wife has planned and led "Ladies' Nights Out" activities. These evenings are for the ladies of our church and they include a meal, some fun, and a brief lesson on being godly women. This has become a wonderful time where Christian ladies can identify with each other and be encouraged and mentored in God's Word together.

Host Saturday night men's prayer meeting. Every Saturday evening since the early days of our church, a group of men gather in the evening to pray for the day to come. In this meeting I share what I am going to preach the next day (By the way, it helps if you know before Saturday night what you are going to preach.), and I encourage them to read through that passage ahead of time. Then I share some special events, progress on the building program, or perhaps some special needs. We pray for other churches, people to be saved, and so much more. The best way to identify spiritually with another man is through getting on your knees with him in prayer and beseeching the Lord for the ministry. This meeting is vital! If only one man attends your prayer meeting, thank God for giving you one godly heart that you can mentor in the faith of Christ.

Host a Men's Leadership Retreat once a year. This is one of my favorite leadership training times. Annually we invite twelve to eighteen new men in our church to a leadership retreat where we invest in their lives and teach them on topics such as prayer, family, local church, time, Baptist distinctives, integrity, and walking with God. God has greatly blessed this retreat over the years and has used it to literally change lives.

Develop a personal discipleship program in the local church. This is one of the best ways to identify with people—helping them grow in the faith. In the early days of our church, all of our personal discipleship was over a coffee table just talking. In recent years we have instituted a much more involved personal discipleship program. The program is about twenty lessons and is conducted by trained "disciplers" who are partnered with new Christians. These people meet weekly to personally work through their lessons and to develop relationships. These loving relationships are critical to helping a new Christian wrestle with new ideas or spiritual concepts that may be foreign to them. Personal discipleship is a vital part of helping someone to understand the Christian faith personally.

There are five purposes for these ways of identifying with people. It is a mentoring process with enormous spiritual implications.

First, you are helping others to know the joy of a committed life to Jesus Christ. It truly is a blessing and a joy to serve Jesus.

Second, you are helping others to see that real Christianity is distinct from the pagan culture around us. We often do not realize how pagan an environment is from which many of our new Christians come.

Third, you are helping new Christians to realize that integrity begins with a personal walk with God.

Fourth, you are showing a new Christian that fellow Christians are available to them and are praying for them. They see the body of Christ at work, and they can sense their own place in the family.

Fifth, you are demonstrating a belief that God is able to do great things through committed people. As you connect personally with people, you are preparing them to reach their full potential for Jesus Christ.

The Impartation of Leaders

There are several areas where new spiritual leaders need instruction. As you begin training national leaders to further the work of Christ, you will need a strategy for training them in the following ways.

1. Instruct them in evangelism. We need to teach and preach about winning souls. I believe that every leader in a church should be a soulwinner. If Jesus said, "Go," I believe that He has said this to the church—to each of us individually. If your leaders are unwilling to win souls, then they should not be placed in a position of leadership.

For many years at Lancaster Baptist, we have conducted TEAM soulwinning training. Any member who is willing to learn how to win a soul to Christ can be instructed through this training course and personally mentored in the process of soulwinning.

2. Instruct them in prayer. We preach and teach about prayer, but we also pray together. Some of the sweetest times of ministry are those times when we gather as a body of believers or as a team of leaders simply to pray. We must teach them to pray because without prayer we can do nothing.

3. Instruct them in the doctrine of the Word of God. We read in 2 Timothy 3:15–16, "*And that from a child thou hast known the holy scriptures, which are able to make thee wise unto salvation through faith which is in Christ Jesus. All scripture is given by inspiration of God, and is profitable for doctrine, for reproof, for correction, for instruction in righteousness.*" We must immediately place new Christians on the right path of theology—from eternal security to the deity of Christ. They need to know the major doctrines of the Word of God.

4. Instruct them in ministry methods. For example, in our Sunday school meetings, in our ushers meetings, in our hospitality meetings, and in our youth ministry meetings we teach our leaders what is expected—times, places, dress, and practical how-to.

It is vital that you clearly define the goals of ministry and that you train your leaders how to accomplish these goals. This practical, how-to training may vary from field to field, but the philosophy of training others to carry out the work should be happening in every field! Teach your workers how to conduct a baptism follow-up visit, how to conduct a class, how to teach a lesson, etc. Servant-hearted people are generally very hungry for this kind of practical instruction, and they will greatly appreciate your training in their lives. We are sometimes very weak in the practical matters of "how-to" ministry. Equipping is not dumping responsibility on the next available body. Equipping is giving practical instruction and personal mentoring in every aspect of ministry.

The Delegation of the Ministry

Maturity does not come with age—it comes with the acceptance of responsibility. There could be people in your church that have been there for twenty-five years yet are still spiritual babes. You may have someone who has been there for five years, and because they are reading, growing, and accepting responsibility, they are ready to serve.

Why is it that we as pastors are afraid to delegate? Why do we fail to give things away? When we first came to Lancaster Baptist Church, Terrie and I did everything. I was the youth pastor, the choir director, the janitor, the pastor, etc. My wife answered the phone, did all the typing, taught all the Sunday school, etc. Yet, as we identified and mentored new leaders there came a time to delegate some of what we were doing.

We often fail to delegate because we are afraid that someone else will not do as good a job or because we do not feel that we have the time to train another. There are many hindrances to delegation, but the simple fact is, God desires for you to delegate some of your responsibilities to others!

As we learned delegation in those early days, we learned that there are people all over the ministry that can do things much better than we could. Why do we not delegate?

First—insecurity. Let us just be honest. We talk about being accepted in the beloved, we counsel about being accepted in the beloved, but we fear that someone might do a better job than we do. We must realize that we hinder the work of God if we do not delegate. It is not my church or your church—it is the Lord's church. God places into that body whom He will and if you thwart them, then you are a hindrance to the Holy Spirit even if you have the title of Pastor on your door.

Second—disorganization. Failure to plan our calendars or manage our time prevents us from training leaders, preparing mentoring times, and planning ministry structure. You can learn to be organized.

Here are some keys to successful delegation…

1. **Remember to mentor and teach before the delegation.**

2. **Give clearly identifiable duties for the given tasks.** They need training, guidelines, maps, tracts, helps. People need to know what is expected. When people get hired in the world, they get a job description. They should get one at the church as well.

3. **Verbalize confidence in the person to whom you delegate.** Catch them doing something right. Let them know that you believe in them. Often, they do not really

believe that God can do something in their lives. Verbalize your confidence.

4. **Give them the authority to get the job done.** There should be guidelines and checks, but give them the freedom to do their job. Let them do what God has called them to do. Your goal should be to put the right person in the right position so that you can give them their job and then get out of the way and let them do their job.

5. **Establish budget limits if applicable.**

6. **Give them room to fail and learn from their mistakes.** I have made a lot of mistakes over the years. Let people learn and grow and make some mistakes.

7. **Set predetermined checkpoints for delegation.** Determine when you will meet with them to review progress, answer questions, and provide oversight.

8. **Give them credit for a job well-done.** Reward and celebrate the godly success of others on your team.

Delegation can be a scary thing. Not long after our oldest daughter got her driver's license, she was traveling with me on a preaching trip, and I decided to let her drive on the way home. Big mistake. It was a near death situation. I kept saying, "Honey, you don't get in the fast lane and then drive fifty miles an hour when there are trucks behind you...."

This was definitely one of those times when delegation was scary! I was coaching, but it was a frightening thing. That is how delegation will often feel. Shortly after you place a new leader into a position, you will be tempted to "grab the wheel" and take back control. Be patient. Give that leader some time and loving mentoring, and eventually God will develop him and multiply your ministry!

The Regulation of Leadership

This thought ties in with the "predetermined checkpoints" that were listed above. As you develop and delegate to new leaders, you will find your role of oversight growing. It is vital that you give godly, biblical oversight of the entire ministry. You must *inspect* what you *expect*. Let me suggest a few ways to regulate what you delegate.

1. **Written reports**—perhaps you could request a written update at given intervals from those in leadership.

2. **Teacher evaluations**—perhaps you could have others evaluate and observe the ministry and work of those whom you have trained.

3. **Regular staff meetings**—perhaps you could have weekly and monthly meetings when you discuss ministry progress and future plans. These are important even if you are working with just a few volunteer laborers.

4. **Individual meetings**—perhaps you would meet one-on-one to evaluate progress, prioritize and strategize together.

As you begin your church on the mission field, it is critical that you have a heart to identify, select, and develop other leaders around you who can take the work of the ministry farther than you could by yourself. The secular world calls this "synergy." Synergy means that the product is greater than the sum of the parts. The principle is that people working together can accomplish more than if they all worked equally as hard, but separately.

God calls it *"striving together for the faith of the gospel."* Biblical ministry was not designed to be a "one man show." God has ordained the work of the church to be "body work"—multiple parts working together for a common purpose of sustaining life.

God does something great through spiritual teams who come together for the purpose of glorifying Him.

Commit yourself on the field to developing leaders. Have a biblical strategy to build others around you and watch how God will greatly bless your efforts!

CHAPTER FOURTEEN

The Enemies of Missions

PAUL CHAPPELL

S ince the early moments of God's plan of redemption, Satan has fought against the spreading of the Gospel. As early as Matthew 4, we read how Satan tempted the Lord Jesus to turn from His mission to seek and to save the lost of this world.

Any individual or church who intends to commit lives, finances, and resources to the cause of reaching the world with the Gospel of Jesus Christ can expect similar trials and temptations from the wicked one. Satan will attempt—through the lust of the flesh, the lust of the eyes, and the pride of life—to redirect you and destroy you as you endeavor to serve the Lord Jesus Christ.

Thankfully, we have many promises in the Scripture that teach us of our victorious position in Christ. The Scriptures teach, *"...greater is he that is in you, than he that is in the world,"* and we thank and praise the Lord for the power He provides as we labor for Him in this needy hour!

Besides the daily darts thrown by Satan against God's people as they endeavor to spread the Gospel, there are several other factors that can be listed as the enemies of missions in the twenty-first century.

Enemy #1—Disobedience

No matter how we attempt to analyze the Great Commission of Matthew 28, it is still a command from Jesus Christ. It is truly amazing how we can call Him our Saviour, our Lord, and our Master, and yet so easily choose to disobey His Great Commission.

In Matthew 28, just before the Lord ascended to Heaven, He gathered His first flock of believers and commissioned them to go into all the world with the Gospel. This commission, preceding Pentecost, was a command that was given with the accompanying promise—*"lo, I am with you alway, even unto the end of the world. Amen."* Obviously, the Lord Jesus gave this commission not only to His original called-out assembly, but also to every other believer who would follow in their steps. Nevertheless, the great majority of churches today are not involving themselves in local evangelism, nor are they greatly involved in worldwide evangelism.

The enemy of disobedience is widely seen in churches across America when it comes to the Great Commission. Pastors must boldly call God's people back to the place of participation and obedience in the areas of soulwinning, missions giving, and mission sending.

Enemy #2—Selfishness

The second enemy of missions is selfishness. In 1 Timothy 3:1–7, the Bible says, *"This is a true saying, If a man desire the office of a bishop, he desireth a good work. A bishop then must be blameless, the husband of one wife, vigilant, sober, of good behaviour, given to hospitality, apt to teach; Not given to wine, no striker, not greedy of filthy lucre; but patient, not a brawler, not covetous; One that ruleth well his own house, having his children in subjection with all gravity; (For if a man know not how to rule his own house, how shall he take care of the church of God?) Not a novice, lest being lifted up with pride he fall into the condemnation of the devil. Moreover he must have a good report of them which are without; lest he fall into reproach and the snare of the devil."*

In these last days we have seen an unprecedented spirit of selfishness when it comes to the need of worldwide missions. Parents who are raising children for the Lord must always remember that children are the heritage of the Lord. What a tragedy when Christian parents say, "I hope my children will not serve God as missionaries." The Bible says that there is no greater joy than to know that our spiritual children are walking in truth. If we truly believe that missionaries are the modern day heroes of the church, parents should consider it an honor that their children would be surrendered toward missions.

Many young people in the average Baptist church today are very selfish when it comes to worldwide missions. A large majority of students are no longer considering Bible college training, which of course, would precede most missionary service. Thank God for those young people who have surrendered their lives to "whatever God wants" for them. Let us as pastors, youth pastors, and parents continually encourage our young people to be yielded to the Lord no matter what the cost!

The Mormon church, with its false and damnable heresies, has instilled within its young people a sense of urgency and commitment that causes them to feel privileged to give two years of missionary service wherever the church might send them. Would it not be a blessing if every Baptist teenager would feel a similar leading in their lives!

This enemy of selfishness has found its way into the hearts of many Christians who are not willing to give of their finances or of their time for short-term missions projects. The Apostle Paul was very clear when speaking to the Philippian church: "*Not because I desire a gift: but I desire fruit that may abound to your account*" (Philippians 4:17). Those Christians who faithfully support missions through their local churches will rejoice throughout eternity for the part they had in bringing lost souls to the Saviour.

Enemy #3—False Excuses

Many false excuses are given today for why we cannot reach forward with soulwinning and missionary endeavors. Sometimes these excuses are sugar-coated with spiritual terms. For example, I recently heard a staff member from a prominent Baptist church state: "We are not as interested in soulwinning as we are in being faithful witnesses." The problem with this statement is that you are not a faithful witness if you are not involved in personal soulwinning.

Others would say that the times are too dangerous to go forth as a missionary. One wonders if these folks have ever studied the Roman culture of the first century to realize how the early Christians hazarded their lives for the Gospel's sake.

Recently, while visiting the city of Rome, I stood in what many consider to be the last prison cell where the Apostle Paul was imprisoned before giving his life as a martyr. Thank God that the great missionary apostle did not focus merely on the danger, but on the needs of people to know Jesus Christ as their Saviour.

Let me be clear. If you desire an excuse, you will find one. What we need in today's missionaries are men and women who will overcome any and every excuse with a fiery heart of faith. We need courageous men and women who will trust that God can and will do a great work through them!

Enemy #4—Ecumenism

Most students of contemporary theology are well aware that there is much doctrinal compromise taking place regarding the faith and practice of Bible-believing Christians in this day.

A recent movement that illustrates this point was "The Promise Keepers" movement. In my book, *The Promise I Cannot Keep*, I shared why I, as a fundamental Baptist pastor, could not promise to "tear down the walls of denominationalism" for the sake of "unity." While I am no fan of denominations, per se, I do believe there are distinctive doctrines that have formulated my position as a Bible-believing Christian.

When the Los Angeles Roman Catholic Archdiocese was invited to participate in The Promise Keepers movement, and when the Mormons became actively involved in the Los Angeles rally, "red flags" began to go up in my heart.

In addition to meetings like the Promise Keepers, we also hear the voices of charismatic television stations telling us that one can receive Christ through the mass and that we must all join together with our Roman Catholic brothers in these last days for fellowship and praise and worship.

These philosophies are the enemies of true biblical missions for the simple fact that if the Roman Catholics are already our brothers, then why would we ever send one more missionary to Mexico, Central, or South America?

The ecumenical movement, along with its doctrines of infiltration, is an enemy to soulwinning missionaries everywhere because it dilutes the truth and blurs the lines of the spiritual battleground where we must stand for the Lord Jesus Christ.

Enemy #5—Calvinism

In recent years there has been a resurgence in the teaching of the doctrines of reformer, John Calvin. While every honest Bible student would agree that we are *"elect according to the foreknowledge of God"* (1 Peter 1:2), and that God in His sovereignty knows who will trust Him and who will not trust Him, there seems to be an extreme brand of Calvinism that is turning many away from soulwinning and worldwide missions in this day.

Great missionary movements of the past went forward under the flag, "whosoever will may come." When one stands at the entrance to Westminster Abbey, he will see the grave marker of the great missionary David Livingstone. On his grave is the verse from John 10:16 which says, *"And other sheep I have, which are not of this fold: them also I must bring, and they shall hear my voice; and there shall be one fold, and one shepherd."* Livingstone often wrote that he felt privileged to preach the blood atonement of Jesus Christ to those enslaved by sin in Africa.

We believe Calvinism has found its way into some independent Baptist churches, who are now emphasizing being a "faithful witness" rather than a confrontational missionary with the Gospel of Jesus Christ. Where would Christianity be if the Apostle Paul had taken this approach?

If a young person were to take Calvinism to its obvious extremes, why would he go to the uttermost parts of the world to be a missionary? I recently read the annual report of a megachurch in Southern California with an attendance in excess of eight thousand per week. They listed in the report forty-six baptisms for the previous twelve months. The pastor is one of the leading Calvinistic theologians in our day, and I believe this report to be an illustration of what Calvinism will do to the evangelistic outreach of a church.

Enemy #6—Satanic Opposition

Finally, at the root of all opposition toward the advancement of the Gospel is the fact that Satan fights every effort of the local church to lift up the Cross of Jesus Christ. Ephesians 6:12 says, *"For we wrestle not against flesh and blood, but against principalities, against powers, against the rulers of the darkness of this world, against spiritual wickedness in high places."*

Whether satanic opposition manifests itself in the form of perverted doctrine, pride, or even assaults against Christians in their efforts to spread the Gospel, we know that Satan is always busy fighting against the work of God. Jesus said, *"...upon this rock I will build my church; and the gates of hell shall not prevail against it"* (Matthew 16:18).

There are many other enemies of missions that could be mentioned, such as the enemies of prayerlessness, laziness, materialism, prejudice, and indifference. While the enemies may be many, and obstacles at times seem more than we can comprehend, it is a great privilege to be a part of God's unfolding plan for worldwide missions. May we instill within the next generation of missionaries a spirit established upon this principle of the Word of God—*"greater is he that is in you, than he that is in the world!"*

CHAPTER FIFTEEN

Reporting and Accountability

PAUL CHAPPELL

In Acts 13, we see the clearest biblical account of the sending and subsequent accountability of the earliest missionaries to their local church.

The focus of the book of Acts prior to chapter thirteen has been on the church of Jerusalem. It was there that the church was empowered, and it was from there that the Christians went out into the surrounding regions with the Gospel of Christ. But in Acts 13, we begin to see the Gospel moving into Asia Minor and Europe.

The focus of the Gospel is now going to move from Palestine, about three hundred miles north to Antioch. It is from Antioch that the worldwide missions program of the first century church will begin. It is from a local church in Antioch that the first missionary journey would be embarked upon by the Apostle Paul.

I believe the major reason for the spreading of the Gospel and the explosive growth of the missions program is because of a man by the name of the Apostle Paul, who was obedient to the Holy

Spirit of God, and because of a local church that knew how to hear the voice of the Holy Spirit of God. We need these types of churches which can still hear the Holy Spirit—He is still speaking!

It is clear in this chapter that the work of missions is local church work—from start to finish. We tend to over complicate matters where God has clearly spoken in Scripture. We tend to create bureaucracies where God simply desires to build His church. The work of local missions should begin and end with the local church—and this will include not only the calling and sending of the missionary, but also the reporting and accountability of the missionary.

Before we visit the subject of accountability, let us remind ourselves of God's model for the foundation of worldwide missions.

The Calling of the Missionary

As has been previously stated in this book, I believe that churches send missionaries, not boards or colleges. In verse two of this chapter we read, *"As they ministered to the Lord, and fasted, the Holy Ghost said, separate me Barnabas and Saul for the work whereunto I have called them."*

The Holy Spirit does the calling. Paul and Barnabas received their commission directly from God. They had been engaged by the Holy Spirit and were now being sent forth from the church at Antioch. The Holy Spirit called, the church concurred with God's calling, and they were sent out to do the work of God. That is wonderful! The only problem is this, the average church today never hears the Spirit in the first place. He is trying to convict of sin and call laborers to serve and witness, yet our spiritual minds are so full of wickedness, busyness, and worldly intentions that we never hear God speak.

The Holy Spirit of God will put the mark of Heaven on a church and yet our flesh will do nothing but push Him away. These people had true spiritual growth—they were living and loving and getting along. And it is in that environment when the Holy Spirit spoke. I do not want my children or our church family to miss the voice of God because we are too caught up in other matters.

The local church heard and sent, which makes the local church the sending agency.

The Accountability of the Missionary

Serving Christ on a foreign field can mean that you and your family are easily detached from your sending and supporting church. This detachment can result in myriad problems—both spiritually and emotionally. The spiritual health of your family, your personal life, and your ministry work could be greatly dependent upon how accountable you choose to be. It is vital as you begin your work abroad, that you maintain a close spiritual connection with your pastor and with those who would give you godly counsel and direction. It is also vital for your supporting churches to see the eternal fruit that is being developed through their faithful giving.

In Acts 14:26–27 we read, *"And thence sailed to Antioch, from whence they had been recommended to the grace of God for the work which they fulfilled. And when they were come, and had gathered the church together, they rehearsed all that God had done with them, and how he had opened the door of faith unto the Gentiles."*

Here we see a wonderful picture of the accountability of the missionaries to the local church from which they have been sent. The Bible is very clear that the first missionaries returned to Antioch and there they rehearsed all the things God had done on their missionary journey.

Many missionaries and missionary groups talk about accountability but do not practice accountability. It has been my experience over the years that Christian men in the ministry, or otherwise, who have asked me about my accountability practices as a pastor have often had very little accountability in their own lives and ministries. Some men who speak against the use of missions boards do so because they do not like the accountability or reporting requirements. (Most missions organizations require a financial reporting sheet to be filled out monthly by the missionaries.)

From this biblical model, I believe that every missionary should desire a strong level of accountability. There are too many opportunities for the devil to tempt, too many opportunities for a missionary to be falsely accused, too many statistics of failure—we must safeguard our integrity and our ministry through accountability. Accountability is not a wall that limits us, but a fence that protects us. We must walk circumspectly as we do the work of the Lord.

First, I believe in personal accountability. This would include accountability regarding your devotional life, your personal walk with God, and your family life. This personal accountability should be made primarily to the home pastor.

For example, the missionaries who are sent from Lancaster Baptist Church send a monthly update of their work and they also share details about their devotional and family lives. Often I will email them if I sense some level of concern.

Second, I believe in financial accountability. Financial stewardship, building programs, and other financial matters could be communicated either through the missions board or directly to the local church leadership. However the information is disseminated between the local church and a missions agency, there should be financial reporting on a regular basis between the missionary and his accountability team.

Third, I believe in ministry accountability. Missionaries should regularly and transparently report to sending and supporting churches regarding the development of the ministry. This could be in the form of a prayer letter or written update. The sending church should be able to rejoice in the fruit that is abounding to their account, and the missionary should feel some sense of responsibility to show spiritual fruit for his labor.

Additionally, I believe the home church should send a pastor or a representative to the fields of the missionaries periodically, if at all possible. This allows the church to feel a part of the work and to see, firsthand, the living conditions of the family and help with any need that might exist.

Because we have several missionaries sent from our church, it would be very difficult for us to handle all of the medical insurance and financial reporting needs. These needs, of course, include the filing of income taxes on an annual basis and many other details. Therefore, most of the financial accountability of our missionaries has been done through missions agencies. I do believe it is important, however, for the sending pastor to be aware of the general support needs of a particular mission field and help ensure that those financial needs of his missionary are being met.

The means for accountability may be as varied as writing letters, sending emails, or even video conferencing through the internet. Whatever means is chosen, the missionary should voluntarily be accountable on a regular basis. The following are some areas with which a missionary should endeavor to be accountable to his sending pastor and accountability team.

1. The missionary should be accountable regarding his personal and spiritual development as a Christian man. In my opinion, this should be shared with his home pastor.

2. The missionary should be accountable regarding his family life and the time he is spending with his wife and children.

3. The missionary should give a financial accountability sheet showing, in general terms, how the monies are

being spent between personal needs and the missionary work needs on a monthly basis.

4. The missionary should involve his home pastor and accountability team in decisions that require major purchases.

5. The missionary should also be accountable to a spiritual advisory team regarding any discrepancies or difficulties he has encountered with other missionaries. These types of difficulties should be kept to a minimum where spiritual missionaries are involved. But when they do develop, it is good to document and be accountable as to his actions in these matters.

6. Finally, I believe that every independent Baptist missionary should be accountable regarding his missions work to every supporting church. I still believe in sending a letter once a month with an update regarding souls that are saved, people who are being discipled, and churches that are being planted.

I realize that this is a cumbersome task for many missionaries, but I also believe it is a common courtesy and something that any hard-working missionary should be willing to do. Our missionaries in Europe may have "less to report" in the sense of souls that are being saved as those who may be ministering in the Philippines; however, every missionary should be working just as hard. They should be putting in the same number of hours and labor for the Lord. Do not ever hesitate to share the number of tracts that have been handed out, the number of Bibles that have been passed out, or the number of times you have attempted to share the Gospel— even though you may not have always seen a conversion.

Remember, the early missionaries rehearsed all that God had done. The Gospel was not always received in every city where Paul went, either. Yet, he rehearsed even the difficulties with the church at Antioch.

Concerning Mission Boards

Over the last few hundred years we have heard much concerning the rise and development of missions agencies or missions boards. Great missionary enterprises have focused on whole continents and people groups, and the result has been the salvation of thousands of souls.

The first missions board was established in 1792, by William Carey in Kettering, England. To be proper in our historical perspective, we must report that the missionary recruiting took place in local churches and the funds for the missionaries came from members of local churches. Even the great missionary, David Livingstone, heard about missions while sitting in a local church in his homeland of Scotland. Similarly, William Carey and other great missionaries who organized cooperative missionary enterprises worked with the support of the local church.

There are some dangers with missions agencies and missions boards. One danger is the doctrinal error that has crept into some agencies. Some of these agencies, like the churches that surround them, do not stand firmly on the fundamentals of the faith and have begun compromising in the areas of personal and ecclesiastical separation.

Another problem is that some agencies have become so heavy in the "bureaucracy of their headquarters" that the missionaries actually receive only a fraction of the money sent in for missions work. This is one reason that I am thankful to be an independent Baptist. Independent Baptist missionaries receive all, or nearly all of the support sent to them, depending upon the way in which it is sent.

Another danger is that these agencies can become heavy with directors or leadership that is not fulfilling a purely missionary enterprise. Sometimes one wonders if titles are being created for retiring missionaries, or missionaries who are unwilling or unable to go back to the fields, simply to keep them on in some advisory capacity as a missionary director or affiliate.

If a director of a missions board is actively involved in raising funds for the field he represents, visiting the mission field often, encouraging missionary families in field conferences, and continuously contacting the home and sending churches with updates and encouragement regarding the missionary, then I thank God for missions directors with the heart to serve in this capacity. The best missions directors are personal soulwinners and are involved in missions work through preaching, raising funds, and encouraging God's servants.

I advocate cooperating with a Bible-believing Baptist missions board if the board states and practices submission to the local churches whom they serve and if the board recognizes that they are a "conduit" of a "service ministry," but not the final authority in the life of a missionary.

I have appreciated my fellowship with Baptist International Missions, Inc. for a number of reasons. First, I am thankful for their strong statements regarding fundamental doctrine and practice. Second, the leadership of this board always defers to the home pastors in matters of missionary personnel needs or even disciplinary issues, such as missionary immorality or family break-up.

In my opinion, as soon as the director or missions agency is aware of these problems, the first call should be to the home pastor. I know this to be the policy of Baptist International Missions, Inc.

There are other good missions agencies that have a similar doctrine and philosophy. While every pastor can share horror stories about a missions agency that failed to meet their expectations of a "service agency," I believe there are good missions agencies available to help young missionaries.

While the local church is always the sending agent, these missions agencies can help support the missionaries with training, monthly prayer letter services, income tax services, etc.

On a side note, there are some fields that will only permit one or two Baptist agencies to have access into the country. In these cases, a missionary may not be able to go from his home church directly to the field. Therefore, in my opinion, there is not a simple "blanket rule" for how every missionary must approach getting to the field. We must work to maintain a right spirit of support amongst our fundamental, Baptist churches and missions agencies—especially once the missionaries arrive on the fields and are on the front lines reaching souls for the Saviour.

As you enter the foreign field, for the sake of your personal life, your family, and your ministry—maintain a high level of accountability. Report frequently and rehearse your victories, your prayer requests, your needs, and your battles. Here at home, we are eager to labor with you in prayer and support, but we need to hear from you and rejoice in what God is using you to accomplish. Do not fear accountability; embrace it, and let God bless and protect you through it!

CHAPTER SIXTEEN

Getting Missionary Kids Ready for College

Paul Chappell & Dwight Tomlinson

M ost resident missionaries go to the field as young adults. This is, of course, not true in all situations, but it is true in the majority. Their children are either young when they move to the foreign field, or they are born in the country to which their parents have been called. In many cases the children of the resident missionary pay a huge price in growing up as a part of their parents' ministry. It is not all negative, however. There are many benefits that these young people have in growing up bilingual, bicultural, and immersed in front-line evangelistic ministry.

There are also unique challenges for the kids who grow up on the mission field. For example, if an American missionary raises his children in Asia, the children may have a very difficult time adjusting to American culture as an adult. Are they Chinese? Of course not, they are American. But the truth is that they may be much more Chinese than American in the way they see themselves and the world around them. They look American, but they think

Chinese. They would much rather have roast duck for lunch than a hamburger. They may not understand American humor or values. They do not get the jokes or the slang expressions that others their age use. They did not grow up with American television or with the many other forces which shape American culture and society. They probably will not even know how different they really are until they return to America without their parents. Many missionary kids find themselves at Bible college surrounded by hundreds of other young people their age, and yet secretly feeling like lonely misfits!

When I (Paul Chappell) returned from Korea as a missionary kid in 1979, several of my fellow missionary kids had also returned at the same time and were on their way to college.

As I shared previously, one close friend of mine had lived in Korea all of his eighteen years and had very infrequently visited the United States. As he settled into his college life in the Pacific Northwest, he soon found himself struggling to relate with his fellow American students. Within two months of beginning his studies in college, my friend, whose parents were still in Korea, committed suicide. In his suicide note he mentioned feeling alone and not knowing how to cope with his life in America.

I do not mean to imply that every missionary child returning to America to live on his own will have serious adjustment issues. No two people are exactly alike, and the issues vary from person to person. Some kids come back to the States, enroll in college, adjust quickly, and go on to immediate success in serving the Lord. Others struggle with these cultural and social adjustment issues, and in some extreme cases the end result has been tragic.

The devil will use anything he can to destroy a life and especially the life of one so uniquely qualified to serve the Lord. Those who have been raised in the homes of godly, full-time servants of Christ have great potential to damage Satan's kingdom, and he will make every attempt to stop them from following in the footsteps of their parents.

It has been my experience after talking to dozens of missionary kids from all over the world, that all of them experienced at least some difficulty adjusting or readjusting to American life—whether in a minor area such as missing the food of their childhood culture or in an extreme feeling of total abandonment "in America." Every missionary kid that I have ever spoken with experienced some form of reverse culture shock when they returned to America on their own.

It is imperative that we give serious consideration and prayer to preparing these precious young people for their return to America. Many missionary kids will be called by God to spend their lives proclaiming the Gospel in their adoptive countries, but even in those cases most will return to the States for preparation. We should not assume that every child raised on a foreign field will be called to remain in that field. Many will return to the States and be led to serve the Lord in other areas and ministries.

Allow us to give some practical suggestions that will hopefully help these "third-culture kids" to adapt into whatever culture the will of God should lead them.

Do Not Lose Your American Identity or Language

Although the missionary must, of necessity, speak the language of the people to whom he is called, it is not necessary or right for their children to lose the ability to function in English. Some missionaries have wisely adopted the rule that English will always be spoken in the home while the native tongue is always to be spoken outside the home. This insures that the children will truly be bilingual. Some missionaries even apply this rule to their children's friends when they are at the house. The friends are expected to speak English while they are visiting in their home, if possible. This rule may need to be modified to fit the individual home, but it is, in our estimation, a very good idea.

Celebrate American Holidays and Include Other Missionary Families

Holidays such as Thanksgiving, Independence Day, and even Christmas may mean nothing to your host country, but they can still be celebrated as special occasions in your home. Teach your children why these occasions are important and what their significance is in American history.

Missionary kids should not lose their appreciation and love for America. If there are other missionary families in the area, perhaps some of these holidays could be celebrated together. Many good ideas for evangelism have been born around a relaxed time of fellowship and food among like-minded missionaries. It was at a Thanksgiving dinner in Hong Kong that I (Dwight Tomlinson) in 1984 had the idea for a missionary/national pastor prayer meeting. That weekly prayer meeting has continued for over two decades and has been used of God to foster a loving and close relationship between the participants.

Be Careful about the Education That Your Children Receive in School

Many missionary families choose to homeschool, which is an excellent option. Some families either cannot or choose not to homeschool. Whatever the case, it is the parent's responsibility to know what their children are being taught and to insure that they are receiving a quality education. If your children are being taught things that you deem incorrect, you have the responsibility to set the record straight. If your children are being taught anti-American views, you should not allow those views to go unchallenged.

The missionary should not preach the virtues of America to his congregation, but he should definitely make sure that his own children understand what a great country they have "back home." We are not called or sent out to make disciples for America. We are called to make disciples for Jesus, but that does not mean that our own children should not know about the greatness of their home country.

When I (Paul Chappell) attended the Seoul Foreign School in Korea, I was exposed to an outstanding academic institution. In fact, the school had been established by Presbyterian missionaries. These types of excellent educational opportunities are available in some lands. Once again, a parent must be involved in the process of education, even if there is a school available. The parents should be aware of the curriculum and the social atmosphere of the school. Just because you are missionaries does not mean you cannot participate in the active development of your child's education.

Keep in Touch with the Preachers, Churches, and Bible Colleges Back Home

Listen to preaching CDs and view the websites of supporting churches back home. This should also include your sending church. It is important that your children have some ministries and preachers that they admire back home. Remember, they may or may not be called to remain on the mission field forever, and if they do return to the States it is important that they have some preestablished ties and that they feel a connection with what God is doing back home. It will help them if they feel an affinity with their home church and pastor. The truth is that they have people back home that love them and are praying for them. There are people back home that are very concerned about their spiritual welfare. It is wrong for them not to know that they are loved and prayed for by family and friends in America.

Recently, while on a foreign mission field in Europe, I (Paul Chappell) met some teenagers in a missionary home. Not only were they beginning to believe some of the European dogma concerning America, but they were also beginning to question the love of the American Christians back home for them. They had not been visited on the field by any supporting pastors, nor had they received care packages or other love gestures from supporting churches. I was glad God gave me the opportunity to reach out to them and remind them that there were many people back home who are proud of our missionaries and praying for them on a daily basis.

Everybody should know that they are loved, especially these young people that will most likely come back and attempt to fit into a place that may seem cold and strange at first. They should know that there are people they can talk to and that will pray with them and encourage them as they make the adjustment to American culture. If possible, make a trip or two back home during the children's teenage years to visit a few Bible colleges. Interview the administration concerning the philosophy and passion of the school for missions and missionary families. This will give you an opportunity to explain some of the unique needs to your young person returning to the States for the first time. It will also give you the opportunity to determine if the administration has a love and burden for missionary kids.

Stay in Touch with the Extended Family Back in America

Staying in touch is easier today than it has ever been. Email and internet phone-calling make it possible for the missionary kids to keep in touch with grandparents and extended family in most parts of the world today.

We would also encourage relatives from the States to visit the foreign field as often as possible. This is especially helpful when the relatives know the Lord and will be a positive influence upon the children concerning the work that God has called the family to do.

Just the other night, I (Paul Chappell) observed one of our Filipino families speaking to Mrs. Curtis Graham, one of our church members, whose son is a missionary in the Philippines. As I approached them, I discovered that our Filipino member was getting ready to visit the Philippines for a few weeks and Mrs. Graham was sending a care package to her son in the Philippines! These types of ongoing communications are greatly needed by every missionary family.

Resist the Temptation to Not Come Home on Furlough or to Leave the Children Behind

Furlough is supposed to be a time of rest, reporting, and raising new support. In reality, furlough is often anything but relaxing or enjoyable. Often the furlough turns out to be much more trouble than its perceived worth. It is important not to be short-sighted concerning the benefits of furlough. The missionary should control his schedule, making sure that there is adequate time for the three objectives mentioned previously, namely rest, reporting, and raising additional support.

Travel is easier today than ever before. Many missionaries are taking more frequent furloughs for shorter periods of time. Traditionally, independent Baptists have observed a rule of thumb of four years on the field, followed by one year at home. This has more of a practical than scriptural foundation. Each situation will be different. The tradition of a one year furlough is often very difficult when considering the fragile nature of a new work and the growth of new Christians. You might consider making use of newer technologies such as video links, web cameras, DVDs, and teleconferencing. These modern technologies make reporting much easier than in years gone by, and they may allow you to stay on the field in a more consistent manner.

Furloughs will be influenced by the needs of the missionary family, the maturity and ability of national leadership, as well as other factors. The point is that furlough should be looked at as a means of preparing teenagers for the inevitable return to America. The goal is to make re-entry into American culture as smooth as possible.

Look at Your Children as an Important and Vital Part of Your Mission Field

Often those of us in "full-time ministry" lose sight of the fact that our immediate families are part of the world that we are commanded to reach. We do not see the inconsistency and sin of ignoring our own children, while expending ourselves in the effort to make disciples of someone else's children. God's Word is very clear that fathers are commanded to win their own children to Christ and raise them to love and serve the Lord (Deuteronomy 6:6–9; Ephesians 6:4).

We find no biblical justification for God's servants disobeying those commands on the pretense of helping others. Someone has wisely said, "It is never right to do wrong, to get an opportunity to do right"! We understand that our children must learn to live for others and that serving Jesus Christ will sometimes require personal sacrifice and flexibility. We are not advocating a selfish home life where we put our family first to the detriment of ministry. That is not Christ-like love. We follow the one who gave up everything to sacrifice Himself on an old rugged cross for an undeserving world. Our children should be introduced to genuine sacrificial love as they see it worked out in the home. What we are encouraging you to have is a balanced, biblical approach to family and ministry.

Be careful of the mistaken idea that there is something unspiritual about caring for your own family. We believe the opposite is true. We are convinced that it is carnal and wicked to ignore God's clear command to love and nurture our own families.

God judged Eli for his failure to minister to and restrain his own sons. God did not excuse Eli from the command to minister to his own family just because he was in full-time ministry. Certainly Eli was expected to minister to the entire nation of Israel as the high priest, but that did not mean he was granted permission to ignore his own sons.

The Bible tells us the sad story of a man whose ministry effectiveness was eroded by the wicked behavior of his own children. Rather than overlooking his failure as a father, God sent a man of God to rebuke and warn Eli (1 Samuel 2:27–36).

Please do not misunderstand our intentions in writing these words. There are no perfect fathers or homes, and our children know that by personal experience. We are simply attempting to give the ministry workaholic permission to go home and tend to his own vineyard. You do not need to feel guilty about spending some time and money on your family. Ask God to help you avoid both unhealthy extremes when it comes to family and ministry. Both are important and one does not have to be sacrificed for the other.

Remember, duties never conflict. God would not ask you to sacrifice your family to save another family. Your children are no less precious to God than someone else's. Our goal should be to reach both.

Choosing a Bible College

Choosing the right Bible college is a critical decision for every family, but especially for the missionary family. Nothing is more important than proving what is the "good and acceptable and perfect will of God" regarding this matter in the life of your child.

We realize that not every missionary child will attend a Bible college, but we believe it is a great credit to our independent Baptist missionaries that a vast majority of our children attend Bible colleges and pursue lives of ministry for the Lord Jesus Christ.

Should your child express a desire to attend a secular college and pursue a career in something other than the ministry, we highly recommend that they be encouraged to attend one year of Bible college in order to lay a foundation for their lives of service to Christ in the years ahead. This year of Bible college is also a critical transitional time for students coming from a foreign culture.

Because this time is so important in the life of your student, we believe it is vital that he find a college that has the right qualities for the missionary child. This should be a college with a nurturing and discipling spirit that is evident and noticeable from the administration all the way to the dorm and room supervisors—strong Christians who will be personally involved in your student's life on a daily basis.

Recent statistics have shown that a vast number of young adults graduating from Christian high schools are falling away from the faith within a few weeks of graduation. Some estimate that today's evangelical churches are only keeping four percent of their young people after high school graduation. If this is true amongst teens in general, we must especially prepare the missionary's children for their re-entry into American culture and into Bible college.

Besides a nurturing environment, the Bible college should be one that most closely aligns with the heart and philosophy of the missionary. In most cases, this will include a heart for souls, a worldwide vision, a commitment to soulwinning, and a solid commitment to the fundamentals of our faith.

Because of the continuing changes taking place in the philosophies of local churches in the States, the missionary should not assume that the college he attended or one that is supported by his particular fellowship is the obvious first choice for his children.

Too often, a college is chosen because of some personal loyalty rather than the clear leading of God. Do not allow institutional loyalty to overrule your commitment to doctrine and a right ministry philosophy. Every parent must give due diligence and prayerful support in helping his children with this important decision.

Many more pages could be written on the subject of choosing a Bible college, but we strongly encourage parents of junior and senior aged children to begin visiting websites, requesting materials, and perhaps plan a Bible college trip for the purpose of looking at the top two or three choices God has laid on their hearts.

Visiting and Growing

Once the decision has been made regarding Bible college, we highly recommend that the parents arrive one or two weeks early, before the beginning of the semester, in order to spend time helping their student adjust and acclimate to the area in which they will live. As a Bible college president, I (Paul Chappell) have been very pleased to see many of our missionary families come early enough to visit the shopping malls, stores, and restaurants in our area. These missionary families have also visited the services of Lancaster Baptist Church and have established relationships with our loving church members who will share the burden of caring for and meeting the needs of missionary kids. We believe this care, on the part of the church family and college staff, is one of the reasons that ten percent of our students are missionaries' children.

One missionary family from Japan recently spent several days here before saying goodbye to their student. While they were here, they took pictures of the church, the dorm, and the shopping areas around town. They told me, "We want to have a picture in our hearts and minds when our daughter calls and tells us about some places she is experiencing while in college."

Many Bible colleges today have a parent orientation. We strongly encourage the missionary parents to attend these orientations, ask questions, and get the contact information necessary from the college administration. Obviously, all provisions for healthcare forms and other medical and legal matters should be discussed with the college administration.

Finally, be sure to have an appointment with the leadership of the Bible college to explain any concerns you have about your student. Most Bible colleges greatly appreciate this level of communication from parents in general.

Keeping in Touch

Keeping in touch has never been easier than it is today. From teleconferencing to video conferencing to email, there are many ways to stay in touch with your student.

As you keep in touch with your child, we recommend that you ask questions that will allow you to have a heartfelt answer from your student. Also, we recommend that you call the college administration every few weeks during the first semester to see if there are any special needs or prayer requests regarding your child. If your home pastor is in the vicinity or someone from your home church has opportunity to visit your child, this is always a great help for homesick students.

Some of the biggest spiritual and emotional hurdles for your child will come during the Thanksgiving and Christmas holidays. If you are fortunate enough to schedule your furlough for their first semester in college, then it is a wonderful thing to join them for the holidays. If this is not a possibility, be sure to make the Bible college staff aware of the situation. It is the tradition of several staff and administration members of West Coast Baptist College to open their homes for students during these holidays. I am sure other colleges have similar programs for missionary students or would be happy to make arrangements for them during these critical times that tend to increase homesickness.

Finally, be sure to request copies of the financial and academic records of your student. These are some obvious indicators as to the adjustment your child is making.

As you prepare your child for Bible college and re-entry into American culture, be ever mindful that the greatest form of communication you can make on behalf of your children is intercessory prayer. How we thank God for the fact that, no matter where we are in the world, we are only one prayer away from our children. May we, as full-time workers for the Lord Jesus Christ, cherish the opportunity to fight the good fight of faith for our children. May we keep in mind that this fight is often won on our knees as we bring our children before the throne of grace, day by day.

CHAPTER SEVENTEEN

Returning from the Foreign Field

PAUL CHAPPELL

The thought of returning from the foreign mission field is normally very difficult for those who have been called to preach the Gospel in a particular land. The cultures and customs of the people have long since become accepted, and the God-sent missionary has grown to love the converts, as well as the lost, in the country where he has served. As we conclude our thoughts, let us spend a few moments considering when and how a missionary should return home to America.

There are at least four categories that must be addressed when considering the matter of returning from the mission field.

Furlough

First, there are times when a missionary must return for furlough. I am aware that the word "furlough" may seem outdated when thinking of a modern missionary endeavor, especially in light of airline travel and other technological advances. However, the need for a missionary to come back to America, from time to time, is vital, regardless of what it is called.

I believe the frequency of someone's return to the States is a matter that should be determined between the local church pastor and the missionary. I have many missionary friends who will come home more frequently and for less amounts of time, and some who will stay on the field for five or six years and come home for as long as a year.

When considering returning to the States for a temporary period of time, there are a few factors you should consider. There is obviously a need for physical rest. Every missionary family deserves a time of vacation and rest just like any other family. In addition, it is normally wise to report to supporting churches to let them see firsthand the work that God is doing. Missionaries with children may also want to schedule a nine-month period home every three or four years, so their children may attend a good Christian school and be better equipped for their re-assimilation into the American culture when it is time for them to go to college. Another consideration for a time of furlough would be for health checkups and other physical needs.

Be sure that you do not plan your work on the field around your furlough. Plan your furlough around your work. Beware of leaving a church just because it is furlough time. Many young churches have been aborted because a missionary left it alone too soon.

I have seen a dangerous trend on the part of some hyper-independent missionaries in recent years. The trend includes traveling back and forth to America so often that they are not establishing real local church ministry and discipling relationships on the foreign field. No pastor or missionary can be greatly used of God unless he spends extended periods of time with the local flock. I am also aware of a few missionaries who claim to be missionaries to a foreign field while they maintain their actual household residence in the United States. I believe these men would be more honest to use a different term, rather than reporting to be full-time missionaries to a foreign field.

The key, once again, to having a proper time of furlough or rejuvenation in the United States is to be highly accountable to the pastor and accountability team with whom the missionary works. I believe it is also wise to write every supporting pastor when there will be any lengthy time spent in the States. Most pastors are very understanding and supportive of these types of needs in the lives of missionary families. It is ethical to be accountable in these matters.

No great missionary ever accomplished a great work without determining to set down roots in his foreign field. Many of our predecessors took their caskets with them as they left America. Others had this similar commitment as they determined to "bury their hearts" on the field. If you are called and if you are passionate about fulfilling your call to foreign soil, you will be compelled by the Spirit of God to set the right balance in this area.

Health Needs

The second reason for returning from the field for an indefinite period is to take care of the health needs of the family. In some situations, it even becomes necessary for a missionary to return from a foreign field due to illness.

Once again, it is very important that a missionary family maintains strong ethics during this transitional period. If coming back to America is intended to be a time when health needs are cared for so the family can return to the field, most pastors will be fine to continue supporting this missionary through the health trial. However, if the missionary has been home for a year or two and does not have a definite plan to return to the field, it is, in my opinion, necessary for the missionary to be relieved of his missionary status and to find ministry work in the States until God would open the door to return to the field.

I know of a few cases in which missionaries have returned to their home churches in the States to work on local staffs perhaps in some bilingual ministries. Meanwhile, they still travel intermittently to the mission field and claim a missionary status regarding their support. I have often questioned the ethics of a pastor who would retain the services of a man who is helping with the vast majority of his time to build up the local church in America, while he is being supported, financially, by dozens of Baptist pastors who believe they are supporting a missionary on the foreign field. In these types of situations, I believe the missionary either needs to return from the foreign field and stay in the States, or make his way back to the foreign field to properly invest the missions support of other churches. The words of the Apostle Paul are appropriate when he said, "This one thing I do…."

Calling from the Holy Spirit

The third reason for returning from the foreign field is a calling from the Holy Spirit to a ministry back in the homeland. There have been times when God has used a man to go to a foreign country, for a time, to establish local churches and to train national workers. Then, through prayer, Bible reading, and counsel, that same man is led of God back to his homeland to continue doing the work of the ministry in some other capacity.

When a man feels he must return home to serve in a ministry in the United States, it is vital that he communicate the timing and purpose of all such transitions to his supporting pastors. A letter to the pastors stating the date the missionary will return to the States is appropriate. I have known of missionaries who have returned to the States and waited several months before notifying supporting pastors that they would no longer be returning to the field. Once again, there is an ethics problem with a missionary who would receive several months of support while being on salary at another ministry in America.

On the other hand, a pastor who loves the work of God should not question a missionary who is returning from the foreign field. He should be glad that they went in the first place and that he had the privilege of supporting them.

Marital or Family Problems

Another reason a missionary may need to return from the foreign field is because of marital or family problems. Even as a pastor is required to have a faithful family life as outlined in 1 Timothy 3, I believe a missionary must also have a faithful family life while training pastors on the foreign field.

In the event that a missionary has children who have become rebellious to the point that the testimony of Christ is being hindered, or if the missionary has had a personal moral failure, it is time to return home to be biblically restored. These are difficult things to discuss, but we would be remiss in our responsibility if we did not mention that from time to time Christian servants must step down from their pulpits in order to become accountable to their sending churches and to be obedient to the Word of God once again.

Death

Finally, some will leave the foreign field by way of death. Recently, while spending some time in England, I visited Spurgeon College. On one of the walls was the following sign:

IN MEMORY OF
SILVESTER FRANK WHITEHOUSE
A BELOVED STUDENT
AND THE FIRST MISSIONARY FROM THIS COLLEGE
TO GAIN THE MARTYR'S CROWN.
SHAN-SI CHINA
JUNE 1900
FAITHFUL UNTO DEATH

In the highly mobile society in which we live, where people are going to and fro, it is my prayer that God will raise up a generation of pastors and missionaries who will find a field and labor in that field until Jesus comes or until He calls them home. May God truly give us a generation of laborers who will gladly expend their lives on the field. May we be willing to pay the price that countless others have paid before us for the faith of the Gospel. Romans 11:29 says, *"For the gifts and calling of God are without repentance."*

While this verse does not limit a person to a single location of ministry, it reminds us of the seriousness of our calling to preach the Gospel of Jesus Christ. May we pray today that our missionary brethren will have God's anointing upon their lives to find the fields of God's choice for them and to stay in those places until revival comes for the glory of God!

CONCLUSION

$\mathbf{M}$atthew 28:18–20 states, *"And Jesus came and spake unto them, saying, All power is given unto me in heaven and in earth. Go ye therefore, and teach all nations, baptizing them in the name of the Father, and of the Son, and of the Holy Ghost: Teaching them to observe all things whatsoever I have commanded you: and, lo, I am with you alway, even unto the end of the world. Amen."*

Again in Acts 1:8 we read, *"But ye shall receive power, after that the Holy Ghost is come upon you: and ye shall be witnesses unto me both in Jerusalem, and in all Judaea, and in Samaria, and unto the uttermost part of the earth."*

What a daunting task and a great commission we have been given—to take the Gospel to all nations—to be witnesses unto the uttermost part of the earth! What a great privilege when we consider that God has chosen us to carry out His mission. He could have chosen the rocks or the trees to deliver His message. He could have commissioned the stars and the mountains to herald the truth of His Son. Yet He chose us! *"What is man, that thou art mindful of him?"* (Psalm 8:4). What a great honor and high calling we have been entrusted with—the ministry of reconciliation—to go to a dying world with the message of life.

As we close this book, may we be reminded that we are not alone in this seemingly daunting task. God has not left us "comfortless" or "powerless"! What a hopeless mission this would be if we were left to our own power and ability. What a desperate and discouraging quest we would face if left to our own strength. Quite the contrary is true.

Jesus Himself promised us that He and all of His power would be with us always and unto the end of the world! Again in Acts we are promised that God would endue us with the power of His Holy Spirit to accomplish this Great Commission.

Do you believe that the same God who empowered the Apostle Paul, that the same Holy Spirit who comforted and strengthened him is in you? Do you believe that God still desires to show His great power in the lives of humble servants like us? He promises that His power can be yours as you commit your life to the Great Commission of Jesus Christ.

Friend, in writing these pages, we do strongly believe that the God of the New Testament is still very much alive and very much desiring to empower men to preach the Gospel to every creature. We believe that He will bless your faith, your commitment, your passion, and your vision to reach a people with the truth of Christ.

It is our sincere prayer that these pages have inspired you, challenged you, equipped you, and encouraged you to go forth with great faith and great confidence in Christ.

God's plan for reaching the world has not changed. He still moves through the foolishness of preaching. He is still building local churches. He is still working through men of God who trust Him and follow His commands.

As you serve Christ on foreign soil, may His power, His favor, and His mighty blessings unfold in your life and ministry. May He protect and bless your family, and may He use your efforts to see a great harvest of souls for the Saviour.

This world desperately needs you and the message you carry. Your enemy is ruthless, but your Heavenly Father is greater! Find your strength, your hope, your provision, and your protection in Him.

May you do God's work God's way—and may you give Him the glory for every victory as you labor in His harvest!

Sincerely,

Pastor Dwight Tomlinson
Pastor Paul Chappell
March, 2007

CHAPTER ONE—**The World's Need and God's Plan**

1. Describe the single act of disobedience that plunged the world into sin.

2. To what institution was the Great Commission given?

3. Describe the origin of the battle that is raging for the souls of men.

4. How is the natural man born into this world?

5. Define the word "missions."

Chapter Two—**What Is It Going to Take to Reach the World?**

1. List and describe one passage from the Bible that commissions us to reach the world.

2. From where should we get our inspiration and our methodology regarding world missions?

3. Describe the change of attitude that must happen in the hearts of Christians before we can reach the world.

4. Describe the change in methodology that must happen in order to reach the world.

5. List two "first century" methods to which we must return in modern day missions efforts.

Chapter Three—**Missionary Qualifications**

1. What is the first qualification of a biblical missionary?

2. What is it that will help any missionary endure the trials and hardships of missionary life?

3. What should a missionary have a clear understanding of before entering the foreign field?

4. List five of the nine major doctrines given that every missionary should understand.

5. Describe some possible ways for a new missionary to have a "measure of success" before entering the field.

CHAPTER FOUR—The Preparation of the Missionary

1. What is the first way given to "prepare" for the work of missions?

2. Describe what it means to prepare for missions by "spending time with Jesus."

3. What is one "silent time" in Paul's life when he was preparing for the work?

4. To whom did Paul serve as an apprentice—who mentored him?

5. What is the best training ground for missionary apprenticeship?

Chapter Five—**The Sending Church**

1. Who or what is the "sending agent" for biblical missions?

2. In what chapter of the Bible do we find a blueprint for world missions?

3. Briefly describe the blueprint for world missions that we see in the chapter named above.

4. List three things every "sending church" should be willing to fulfill for their missionaries.

5. List some ways a sending church can help as a reference.

Chapter Six—**Deputation**

1. By the one-hundredth anniversary of Adoniram Judson's death, approximately how many Christians were there in Burma?

2. Define the word "deputation."

3. List the key benefits of deputation.

4. What are some key considerations as you begin deputation?

5. List the four steps to arranging meetings while on deputation.

CHAPTER SEVEN—**Your Supporting Churches**

1. Why did Paul not receive a salary from the church at Corinth?

2. In what two ways was Paul financially supported?

3. List the six responsibilities of a missionary to his supporting churches.

4. List the seven responsibilities of a supporting church to a missionary.

5. What are some good reasons that churches should consider supporting fewer missionaries with larger amounts?

CHAPTER EIGHT—**Arrival and Initial Ministry**

1. What chapter of the Bible gives us an excellent picture of initial ministry on the field?

2. List three or four things that you should do immediately when you arrive on the foreign field.

3. As you get settled on the field, what is the most important thing to remember?

4. What should all ministry have at its heart?

5. Describe some ways in which you may have to be flexible regarding how you start your initial ministry?

Chapter Nine—**Missionary Relationships**

1. Regarding our relationships with other missionaries, how did the early churches send out missionaries?

2. Describe the benefits of working with other missionaries.

3. List the four practical guidelines given for relating and working with other missionaries.

4. What does your ethics reveal?

5. What three questions should you ask before engaging in criticism of others?

Chapter Ten—**Learning the Language**

1. Fill in the blank: It all boils down to _____
    _____.

2. What is the first thing you must do to learn a new language?

3. What is one temptation you will face in learning a new language?

4. What should you insist on from your national workers?

5. List the six obstacles to learning a new language.

CHAPTER ELEVEN—**Culture Shock**

1. List the initial ways you will most likely experience culture shock.

2. What will learning new customs and culture require of you?

3. Complete this sentence: It is not your responsibility to transport _____ _____.

4. What is the first recommendation for overcoming culture shock?

5. How can establishing your home as an American home help with leading your family through culture shock?

Chapter Twelve—**Church Planting**

1. What three things define an indigenous church?

2. Define the difference between a pastor and a missionary.

3. What is the first step to starting a new church?

4. List five of the many priorities you will have to address as you start a new church.

5. What is the best textbook for planting churches on foreign soil?

Chapter Thirteen—**Training National Workers**

1. List one passage of Scripture that teaches us that we are to train other leaders.

2. List the six guidelines for selecting new leaders.

3. What are some ways that leaders can connect and identify with people?

4. What should you teach your developing leaders?

5. Explain why we fail to delegate, and list three ways you can regulate what you delegate.

Chapter Fourteen—The Enemies of Missions

1. What can any church or missionary who is striving to reach the world with the Gospel expect?

2. List the six primary enemies of missions.

3. Finish this sentence: If you desire an excuse _____
   _____.

4. Explain why ecumenism is an enemy to true biblical missions.

5. List one verse to claim as you confront the enemies of missions in your own heart and life.

Chapter Fifteen—Reporting and Accountability

1. Upon what is your spiritual health and ministry health greatly dependent?

2. To whom should you remain personally accountable for your walk with the Lord?

3. To whom should you remain accountable regarding your finances and ministry?

4. List the six areas in which you should strive to be accountable.

5. What are some potential areas of concern as you choose a missions agency?

CHAPTER SIXTEEN—**Getting Missionary Kids Ready for College**

1. How many missionary kids face difficulties re-entering American culture?

2. What are some good ways not to lose your American culture while on the field?

3. How can you work to keep in touch with pastors and churches in America?

4. What temptation should you resist in regards to time on the field?

5. How should you view your family and your ministry?

CHAPTER SEVENTEEN—**Returning from the Foreign Field**

1. What two extremes must you guard against when considering how often to return to the States?

2. What are the primary purposes of furlough?

3. List the primary reasons missionaries should return home from the field.

4. No great missionary ever accomplished a great work without doing what?

5. How should you approach an indefinite return home with your supporting churches?

Visit us online

striving together.com

dailyintheword.org

wcbc.edu

lancasterbaptist.org

It's a Wonderful Life
In these pages, Terrie Chappell shares a practical, biblical approach to loving your family and serving Jesus Christ. Her humorous and down-to-earth insight will encourage your heart and equip you to love the life to which God has called you. (280 Pages, Hardback)

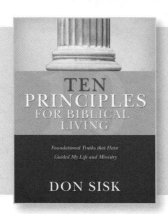

Ten Principles for Biblical Living
Drawing from over fifty-two years of ministry experience and a profound impact on worldwide missions, Dr. Don Sisk shares ten biblical and practical principles that have shaped his life and ministry. These principles will call you to a renewed life of service for Jesus Christ and are perfect for sharing with others as well. (120 Pages, Hardback)

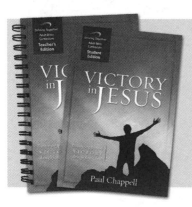

Victory in Jesus
Teacher's and Student's Edition
In these lessons, your students will discover God's purpose for suffering and His method for overcoming trials. They will learn how to face adversity in the light of God's Word and live a victorious and fulfilling Christian life!

done.
Specifically created to be placed into the hands of an unsaved person and a perfect gift for first-time church visitors, this new mini book explains the Gospel in crystal clear terms. The reader will journey step by step through biblical reasoning that concludes at the Cross and a moment of decision. This tool will empower your whole church family to share the Gospel with anyone! (100 Pages, Mini Paperback)

Your Pastor and You
Wise Christians find and establish strong relationships with godly pastors and choose to fight for those relationships. They encourage their pastor, accept his spiritual watchcare in their lives, and support him in his call to serve God. (48 Pages, Mini Paperback)

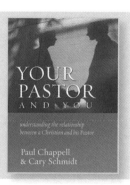

A Maze of Grace
If you or someone you love is enduring a season of suffering, this booklet will provide a cup of fresh water for the journey. Each chapter shares God's wisdom, encouragement, and insight. Each turn of the page will bring fresh hope and trust in the unseen hand of a loving God. (64 Pages, Mini Paperback)

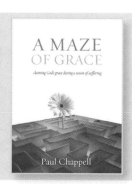